KITCHEN FUGUE

BOOKS BY

Sheila Kaye-Smith

NOVELS
Tambourine, Trumpet and Drum
The Secret Son
Ember Lane
The Valiant Woman
Rose Deeprose
Gallybird
Superstition Corner
Gipsy Waggon
Susan Spray
Shepherds in Sackcloth
The Village Doctor
Iron and Smoke
The George and the Crown
The End of the House of Alard
Joanna Godden
Green Apple Harvest
Tamarisk Town
Little England
The Challenge of Sirius
Sussex Gorse
Three Against the World
Isle of Thorns
Spell Land
Starbrace
The Tramping Methodist

BELLES LETTRES
The Mirror of the Months
Three Ways Home
Speaking of Jane Austen
Kitchen Fugue

VERSE
Saints in Sussex

SHORT STORIES
Selina Is Older
Summer Holiday
Joanna Godden Married
Faithful Stranger

KITCHEN FUGUE

BY

Sheila Kaye-Smith

HARPER & BROTHERS PUBLISHERS

New York *and* London

1945

CONTENTS

84885

KITCHEN FUGUE

Part I

The Subject and the Answer

1.

THIS IS NOT A BOOK FOR THOSE WITH MINDS ABOVE SMALL things. Some years ago I was chidden by a reviewer for writing my religious autobiography without once mentioning either Hitler or Mussolini. I have not been able to keep the former entirely out of this, but I state in advance that I do not propose to give as much space to his activities as to my own.

Throughout the war I have lived in a part of England that has been considered, geographically, the front line. When I began to write this book the German Army was about forty-two miles away and sending over tokens of its presence at Teutonically regular intervals. But even this did not inspire me to write about war, except as it inevitably concerns my subject, which is cooking in wartime—rather, I should say, under war conditions, for peace does not have the same immediate effect in the kitchen as on the battlefield. A certain number of other things will intrude, because food has for me too many associations in life and memory to be isolated as a subject. But though there will be episodes, the subject will return as inevitably as in a fugue.

We all know that Adam was created out of the dust of the earth—the evidence is to be found in the mechanism of his body, which is a factory perfectly designed for the transforming of that dust into himself. His eyes, his nose, his tongue, his teeth, his gullet, his stomach, his bowels, his lungs, his heart, are all so many machines for the different processes of its conversion into flesh and blood. Through his food Adam becomes the world in which he lives—its animals, birds, fruits, grain and leaves, its gases, chemicals and crystals. Just as his soul is the image of God, so his body is the image of the world, and he stands between heaven and earth a micro-cosm of both.

Unfortunately Adam did not appreciate this honor-able position, but tried to improve it by a cheap short cut to knowledge, which, like most knowledge adver-tised as unobtainable by easy methods, proved illusory and brought nothing but trouble both to himself and to the earth he represented. "Cursed is the ground for thy sake," and "by the sweat of thy face shalt thou eat thy bread" . . . what should have been a joyous, effort-less repast became the wages of toil. No wonder that food lost honor with the rest of life, and had, with the rest of life, to be redeemed.

Food is not, however, to be blamed for the Fall. Mother Eve did not eat of the forbidden tree only "be-cause she saw that it was good for food," but also because it was "pleasant to the eyes and a tree to be desired to make one wise." In other words, it was her aesthetic per-ceptions and her scientific curiosity—her higher rather than her lower nature—that led her astray. Nor was food, like clothing, one of the direct consequences of the Fall. Presumably Adam and Eve had been free to eat the fruits of all the trees in Eden except one, and we can picture their eating and drinking very much as in Mr. C. S. Lewis' unfallen planetary paradise of Perelandra, where nature apparently provides a delicious variety of refreshment at no more trouble than the plucking.

In other words, though food is not the result of the Fall, cooking most probably is—like other laborious processes by which we earn what was no doubt originally intended as a gift. "By the sweat of thy face" has a special application to the cook, who wears the sweat rag of humiliation even more necessarily than the lofty cap of pride.

This book is mainly concerned with food in its fallen state—i.e. cooked. In fact my original idea had been to write a cookery book—a Mug's Cookery Book, designed for those who like myself have been forced to take up cooking under every possible disadvantage of ignorance, inexperience, and lack of proper materials. No cookery book that I have ever seen, however elementary, is really what I and those others need. We start not from zero but from frozen depths of ignorance which no thermometer records, and it seems almost a necessity that our mistakes should not be wasted on ourselves and our long-suffering families but pooled for the national good.

But I soon came to see the limitations of my subject or rather of my public. The number of mugs must always be small, because—unless hopeless cases which no cookery book can save—they must inevitably cease in time to be mugs. They must achieve at least the capacity to follow any wartime recipe, such as have been showered upon them by the Ministry of Food, by the press and by the proprietors of advertised goods no longer in general supply. They must even eventually come to the point of being able to adapt peacetime recipes to wartime scarcities. Moreover, almost every woman goes through a different course of experiment—according to her opportunities and according to her tastes and those of her victims.

I have now been cooking for three years, but I have never made a steamed pudding, because my victim and I do not care for such things. Or rather we do not care for them enough to devote our scanty rations of fat and sugar to their creation. A cookery book which ignored puddings would not, I believe, be considered worth its paper allowance by the average woman—who prefers to graduate via the stillroom instead of, as I did, through the scullery. I started off with rabbit stew . . . which brings me to another objection.

As I live in the country I have sources of supply—of

white, innocent supply—which to the town dweller (the majority of readers) could mean only the black market. I have unlimited supplies of vegetables and nearly unlimited supplies of rabbits and of eggs. Only those in the same circumstances will want to know what I do with them.

So my cookery book—like my first attempt at spinach —has boiled down to about a fifth of my original intentions. I have confined it to a single chapter, intended for any reformable mugs that may still exist and have larders not too unlike my own. The rest is, not silence, but a lot of talking.

2.

As a child I was very much greedier than I believe children are today, no doubt for the reason that I was not so pleasantly fed. The late Victorian nursery, though less Spartan than earlier in the reign, did not aspire to the dietetic standards of the drawing room. Certainly there was no thought of its being privileged above the drawing room, and I cannot imagine a Victorian child's ration book (in some unimaginable Victorian total war) entitling him or her as now, to luxuries withheld from what were then called Elders and Betters.

Perhaps it is the modern scarcity of children which has made us study their diet more sympathetically. On the other hand I cannot say that my child contemporaries of the middle class were any less healthy than their descendants today. The privation of what would now be considered the essentials of a balanced diet (I remember looking forward to "jam night" as a treat) does not seem to have made much difference. We had no more colds or infectious diseases than modern children, and, it seems to me, fewer serious ailments such as mastoid abscess or appendicitis.

The fact was, of course, that though our elders had probably never heard of vitamins, the plain food of the period was of a quality that it has never equalled since

—that it had lost long before this last war or even its predecessor. A slice of Victorian bread, baked at some small local bakery, if not in the home itself and spread with butter sent in from some neighboring farm, would be a treat almost unobtainable by any town dweller today. Our present emasculated white loaf is far more like its wartime substitute than its nineteenth century ancestor. We children were never, of course—except by delicious accident—allowed to eat new bread, but that old-fashioned loaf had to be very stale indeed before it became as tough and tasteless as a fresh loaf today.

I did not, however, realize how greatly I was favored, nor could I then have believed that the time would come when a slice of homemade bread and farmhouse butter would charm my memory more nostalgically than any cake or bun. In those days a slice of bread and butter was the inescapable prelude to cake at children's tea parties. Indeed there were some families where the children had to eat two. I shall not forget my surprise when, helping at a children's party after I was grown-up I found that quite a number of my charges definitely preferred bread and butter to anything that came afterwards. No doubt they had plenty of cake at home.

We had cake only on Sundays and at parties, and then only after the assessed quantity of bread and butter had been consumed. But there was one house where the "bread and butter first" rule did not operate, where one plunged joyfully and freely into the full delights of a well-spread table, and that was a house where there were no children at all.

Two doors down our street lived a family of middle-aged spinsters, with their father and mother. There were four Miss Coles—Gertrude, Arabella, Gladys and Edith—and I suppose that their ages ran from thirty-five or so to forty-five, but to me they were ageless, neither old nor young. Their parents certainly were old, with all the emphasis of their period—Mrs. Cole with white hair and a lace cap, Mr. Cole with muttonchop whiskers and a bald head. It never occurred to me to wonder why none of "the girls"—as their father and mother still called them—had married. But when I recall their faces—which survive in my memory as a composite picture of red, eruptive skin and gleaming, steel-rimmed spectacles—I realize that though those faces were not their only fortune, they must have been a heavy charge on the few thousand pounds that their father—a retired insurance broker—might be able to leave among them.

Arabella was the ruling sister, though neither the eldest nor the youngest, and it was she who presided at the tea parties to which my small sister and I would go once or twice a month with the highest expectations of delight. No family of children could compete with her in attraction, for children were always potential rivals and their nurses potential tyrants. Going out to tea with our contemporaries might lead to all sorts of frustrations and humiliations; not so "tea with Arabella," where pride, appetite and freedom were all equally sure of their rights.

At her house we were allowed to do exactly as we pleased—even to the point of going straight home again if we fancied it. This was never a choice of mine, but my sister was prone to sudden fits of homesickness, even at two doors down the road. This had more than once led to trouble with her hostesses at children's parties, as she was too small to go home by herself (or even with me, could my detachment from the revels have been made with any less outcry than her detention) and there was seldom anybody available to send with her. But Arabella would immediately put on her hat and jacket —necessary in those days even for the ten yards' walk between our houses—and whisk her away without any fuss. Moira never refused to go to tea with Arabella— as she refused to go to so many places. She even once went to stay with her, but as, in spite of all the luggage she took, the visit did not last above two hours, it can hardly be considered a departure from custom.

As for me, I did not care who went home as long as it

was not I. When actually the time came my woe was softened by the fact that I carried away with me in a paper bag all those good things I had been physically unable to consume at teatime. My mother once told me that she was never more ashamed of me in her life than when, in response to my own demand, this custom started. But she did nothing to stop it. Perhaps she was thankful for the guarantee it gave of my peaceful return.

The kindly spinster was to be trusted, too, with the digestions of little girls. Though all common restraints had been removed I do not remember tea at Arabella's ever leading to one of those midnight upheavals which from time to time brought an element of sensation into the monotony of nursery life. My tastes were not exotic and quite sufficiently thrilled by Swiss buns, coated with soft white sugar, or—as a crowning treat—by chocolate macaroons on which nested a tiny sugar bird. There would always be a plate of rusks for Moira—a preference for which I despised her heartily.

As soon as tea was over the second part of the entertainment was due to begin. The table would be cleared by the magpie parlormaid; Mr. and Mrs. Cole would withdraw, and generally also the other sisters, leaving us alone with Arabella.

Moira, if her guest head had survived so far, would be read to out of some dull book—she was supposed to like fairy stories, a cult I despised as much as I despised her rusks. But for me, another feast was spread—an intellectual feast this time. The History Books would be laid out on the table, now no longer white under damask but red under baize. I do not know who had written The History Books, which were infinite in number and overwhelming in size. They were certainly not written for children, being very closely printed in a number of dark columns with only a few, quite documentary, illustrations. But for me they were the perfect escape, the perfect franchise.

I would brood over them for as long as I was allowed to stay, pursuing through their dark print, incomprehensible language and bewildering information the light of my hero—struggling to see him more clearly and coming through all obstacles to love him more dearly. My imagination fed by mind and heart was as greedy as my stomach. If asked to choose between those history books and the tea itself I should have been hard put to it for a decision. Mercifully it was never asked for.

I read history at Arabella's for three years, during which I had three heroes in succession. Looking back on them now I feel a little ashamed of them—they are on the whole a sorry lot. The earliest was King Charles I, whose acquaintance I had made in *Little Arthur's History of England*. Here he was romantically illustrated in the act of saying good-by to his children before his head was cut off. If I remember rightly, which it is always possible that I do not, the attitude of The History Books was republican. But that did not influence me. All I wanted was that tragic story of the White King, husband of Queen Henrietta Maria, just as my father was the husband of my mother—father of Charles, James, Elizabeth and Henry, just as my father was mine and Moira's. Somehow I managed every fortnight or so to drag that story out of the darkness of inimical information and gloat over it for an hour, till it was time to take it away with my bag of buns and put it in my dreams.

I clung to Charles I as a hero till his image was dissolved by the Victorian novelist Edna Lyall in her novel *To Right the Wrong*. This book, which entirely captured my schoolgirl's fancy, was romantically republican in sentiment, and my allegiance underwent a corresponding change. I did not, however, put Oliver Cromwell in the dethroned monarch's place. Had he not a wart on his nose?

Charles's heir in my studies and affections was his unofficial grandson, James Duke of Monmouth. Here indeed I was on the liberal side of politics, but not consciously, for my choice had been fixed only by the knowledge that the duke was strikingly handsome as well as romantically unfortunate. I asked no more of a hero than that he should be handsome and unfortunate, though as I grew older I made some efforts to stiffen in my imagination the rather spineless characters I had chosen to adore. Certainly Monmouth played no heroic part in The History Books and my main effort was concentrated on proving him—to my own satisfaction—the rightful heir to the throne. I was convinced of this by the fact that the book declared him the natural son of Charles II. If natural, I argued, he surely could not be as I had seen him described elsewhere—illegitimate. Illegitimate children were not born naturally, but were smuggled by unscrupulous doctors and servants into houses where they did not belong. Monmouth's birth had been entirely natural—he had a father and mother, Charles II and Lucy Waters. Q.E.D.

However, his reign in my heart was a short one, to be succeeded by the longest of all, that of Charles Edward Stuart, the Young Pretender. My first visit to Scotland plunged me into a welter of Jacobite allegiance which I did not climb out of for years. I was now twelve years old, and pictures—including the portraits of my heroes —were beginning to have backgrounds. For three years (when our Scottish visits ceased for the time being) my heart was in a frenzy of devotion not only to the latter house of Stuart, but to the lovely background of its eclipse—to the blue stencil of the Highland hills beyond Perth, the cloud-hung rocks of Glen Affric and Strathmore, the cliffs of Mam Soul and the little snow-filled corries of the Cairn Gorms.

I no longer pursued my hero through the darkness of old-fashioned history. I dragged him out of it into a new home which I built for him myself out of my own knowledge and imagination. I made him the hero of innumerable tales, some of them full-length novels, all lost now except for scraps still littering the attics of memory. By the time I had done with him I was grown-up, writing my first grown-up, published novel, having sailed through the seas of adolescence so powerfully protected by my own mental life that I had not made even a tentative shipwreck on any of those rocks that threaten the romantically addicted young.

3.

DEAR ARABELLA! DEAR, GOOD, KIND, THOUGHTFUL, unselfish, ugly Arabella! I am afraid that I never appreciated her as she deserved. At the time of her tea parties I did not think how much I owed her or wonder why an unmarried, middle-aged woman should spend herself with such generosity and understanding on a not too attractive child. As I grew older and able to make social contacts of my own, I came, I fear, to despise her feasts. Physically I was no longer to be bribed, even at last by chocolate éclairs and cream buns, and mentally I now had a wider and more glamorous range than that provided by The History Books.

When Arabella died of cancer just before the last war, she left those books to me in her will and they took their places on my shelves, among the George Borrows and the William Blakes, the Fieldings, the Richardsons, and the Jane Austens which were all my reading then. They stayed forgotten until the contents of the house were sold on my mother's death, when they disappeared—to delight some other eager romantic child? I doubt it. As for me, I had not even opened them since they became mine, and I still—incredible as it seems—have no idea who wrote them, who planted those dark forests of print through which my mind went crashing in pursuit of a hero.

But though the outward signs have altered there has been no real change in the signified. I still have those two greeds which I satisfied in Arabella's dining room, though they are both, I trust, by this time sublimated. Ever since those days I have found myself enticed by two quite different types of experience, no longer now of buns and heroes but of what might be called the contingent and the noncontingent sides of life. Strictly speaking my twofold indulgence at Arabella's did not bring out this contrast, for in their different way heroes are as contingent as buns. But they suggest at least a duality of interest, neither of which requires to be gratified at the expense of the other.

I have never found that my interest in religion and philosophy (successor to the heroes) has in any way reduced my interest in food, drink, clothes, and the more superficial side of life (successor to the buns). On the contrary, these two interests seem to have stimulated and enriched each other, like the subject and the answer of a fugue. I cannot imagine my life without both of them.

At Arabella's I learned the fallacy of the old antithesis between plain living and high thinking. Her table provided both a carnal and an intellectual feast—it was merely a question of changing the cloth. At Arabella's I both lived and thought my highest, and it has been my almost unqualified experience that those who live plain (from choice) generally think plain too. Certainly I find that the more intelligent of my friends have not concentrated their intellects on abstractions. The scholastic, academic, specialist type may do so, but a normally diffused intelligence will not only light up the study but shed its beams on the dining room and the kitchen.

4.

THERE IS OF COURSE A NATIONAL TYPE WHICH DESPISES all this. I do not mean that there are no citizens of other countries who are indifferent to the physical arts of living, but I know of no other country where to boast of being indifferent to food or ignorant of the ways of preparing it would not be regarded as a first-class proof of imbecility. Certainly no one would lay any claim to virtue on the strength of it. It is only here in this island that food has no place among the creditable interests of life, and those who enjoy it—or would like to enjoy it—must face even now the charge of being gross and low.

An instance of this was the cry raised early in the war against the type of meal provided in certain restaurants. An agitation was started against those who dined expensively in public, and certain reforms were introduced, as a result of which those who dined expensively continued to do so under the moral safeguard that the meal was as like as possible to those they had been forced to eat at their schoolroom dinner tables. This apparently satisfied the critics, for the matter was dropped forthwith. Rich men continued to eat expensively in restaurants and restaurateurs continued to make money, but as the food was as bad as anywhere else no one worried any more. The public conscience was appeased.

This is an inevitable part of the system of "leveling down" which is one of the more regrettable aspects of a half-baked democracy. The only two really democratic countries in the world have not succumbed to it—at least to the same extent—and it is to be hoped that in less agitated times our own quasi-democratic country may realize its drawbacks.

In a true democracy the tendency should be for levels to rise. Human beings naturally want and try to improve their lot, and where the government is genuinely by the people—instead of disingenuously "for the people"—they will be able to do so. Only in places where their power is not genuine, but delegated either to bureaucracy or to a professional proletariat, will there be a tendency to force down standards to a level attainable by anyone who is not a perfect fool.

I have two examples in my mind of the "leveling-up" process. The first comes from prewar France and the scene in Deauville. An expensive relative of mine is strolling by the shore, uncertain where to lunch. He has tried and wearied of all the principal restaurants in the town. But suddenly an odor creeps to his nostrils from seaward—an odor of good fare. Nothing stands between him and the sea but a row of bathing machines. From

·[12]·

them alone can steal this enticing savor. He goes down the wind to meet it and finds at this moment of time and tide that all the bathing machines are empty except one. Here sits the bathing-machine attendant, taking advantage of the general slackness to eat his midday meal, a hot meal which he spoons out of an earthenware casserole.

Does *monsieur* want to bathe?—the tide is not favorable. No, *monsieur* only wants to know what you are eating. *Mon dîner, monsieur.* I know that, but who cooked it? *Ma femme, bien sûr.* Would your wife cook me a dinner like that if I came here at this time tomorrow? The Frenchman perfectly understands and appreciates the compliment.

The next day my expensive relative dined with the bathing-machine attendant, at what price I do not know, but he declares that the meal was as good and well-cooked as any that he had eaten at the local restaurants.

Now I would guarantee that the entire sea front of England could be combed in vain for a bathing-machine attendant who "ate well," as they say in France. A sausage cooked over a primus and a bottle of cold tea would probably be the best he could offer any straying *bon viveur*. And in spite of this he would almost certainly be a richer man than his French counterpart and have in general, a higher, that is to say more expensive, standard of living. But the British workingman is accustomed to (and on the whole satisfied with) devitalized, tasteless, badly cooked food and all he asks is that the bosses shall eat the same.

My other example comes from the United States. I am waiting on the platform at Atlanta, Georgia, and the big locomotive steams in. As it pulls up, the engine driver leans out of it, propping his arms on the edge of the cab. He wears leather gloves, with gauntlets reaching almost to the elbow.

I at once idiotically ask the reason and am told that the reason he wears gloves is because he wants to keep his hands clean. He considers that he has as much right to clean hands as any of the bosses. When he comes off the job he can take off his gloves and his overalls and go with his wife to the movies as clean and spruce as any clerk or doctor. I doubt if his British counterpart would even want to be clean to that extent. He would regard dirty hands as an inevitable consequence of his work, if not a definite badge of honor. He might even despise the clean hands of the bosses. He would probably say that engine driving is a job that cannot be done with gloves on.

Whatsoever may be his reactions they do not take the form of any protection from dirt, and as a result his skin must be so impregnated with soot and oil that it can have no more hope than Lady Macbeth's from the normal processes of soap and water. I have never returned to England from abroad without a general impression of dirty hands, and not necessarily the hands of those who drive engines. Hands grimed by honest toil are one of our national badges of democracy and I live in apprehension of the day when they will be required of all of us.

The drawback to any leveling-up process is that you cannot (at least at the start) impose it on everyone, and for a time you must run the risk of seeing some others better off than yourself. This apparently is just what human nature cannot bear. In all those touching, thrilling war stories of the adventures of shipwrecked men and women in open boats there is one recurrent fact, second only in impressiveness to the heroism of the survivors. That fact is that human beings will suffer almost any hardship as long as they are quite sure that it is being suffered by everyone alike—that, in this case, everything is being shared equally and that no one has the advantage of a single drop or crumb. If the smallest suspicion arises that anyone for any reason is a fraction better off than anyone else, then follows murmuring and even mutiny till absolute equality is restored.

Of course in this particular situation only leveling-down is possible, and it might be wise to consider the whole population of this country in wartime as being in an open boat. A common emergency, a common stringency, a common fear may justify our suspicious glances at our fellow passengers, our determination that none of them shall have anything which we have not got ourselves. But for heaven's sake do not let us call it democracy or imagine that a progressive and happy society can be built up in such a way. If this is democracy then there are no more consistent democrats than cats and children.

When I give my two cats their dinner the same thing always happens—each before beginning his meal glares in stern inquiry at the other's plate. Plainly each is asking—"Has Nikolous, has Tuesday, got more than I have? If he has he'd better hand it over." I do my best to distribute the fare impartially, but sometimes I have erred through ignorance of the exact quantity of nourishment left on a bone, and then I have to listen to the bluest of language while the matter is discussed between "have" and "have not."

When we were children, my sister and I were very like those cats. I could not bear to see her eating her rightful share of any delicacy after I had wolfed mine. Nor could she bear to see me doing the same thing. So we invented a rite called "the last mouthful," which involved the simultaneous consumption of the last fragment of whatever it was. But even this did not bring peace, for there was nothing in the covenant to prevent one of the parties pouching the dainty for just as long as it would remain undissolved. So the act was revised to include a scheduled order of mastication and a simultaneous swallowing.

In animals and children we do not call this equality— we call it envy; and it might be worth trying some day to build up a system in which envy does not flourish. Most of our efforts in the past to adjust the stupid inequalities of our civilization have been wrecked by that very same envy, which has not only inspired the motives but dictated the methods of reform.

Certainly wealth, health, leisure and education, and a great many other good things are most unfairly distributed among us. But none of these is really in short supply, so for a fair division there is no need to dole them out in ounces. We should all of us have as many pounds of them all as we can carry. I hope (though I cannot truthfully say I expect) to see the day when we shall all eat well, that is to say, intelligently, avoiding not only a surfeit of lampreys but a surfeit of fish and chips—a day when our bodies shall all be clean, not because we do no dirty work but because we hate dirt and know how to get the better of it—a day when we shall all keep well because we are neither coddled nor neglected—a day when we shall all be intelligent and enlightened because (no longer blinded by either privilege or envy) we shall have realized that the education given at our public schools is as bad as any other and some totally new form of teaching and learning must be evolved if mankind is to end its history without at least nine tenths of its brain out of action.

Till that day dawns it might help us to anticipate it by following the gaze of Thomas Traherne's *Infant Eye* —a gaze so devoid of envy that it possessed its owner of all that it saw others enjoy.

> For property itself was mine,
>   And hedges, ornaments,
> Walls, houses, coffers and their rich contents
>   To make me rich combine.
> Clothes, costly jewels, laces, I esteemed
>   My wealth by others worn,
> For me they all to wear them seemed,
>   When I was born.

5.

WE SEEM TO HAVE MOVED SOME WAY FROM OUR original subject, but it is not really so very far. Three steps will take us back—cooks, kitchen, food. But did we ever mention cooks? Yes—indirectly—in our quotation from Traherne. I do not suppose that he was thinking of cooks when he wrote: "My wealth by others worn"—but that is exactly what they are to me.

I can contemplate other women's cooks with satisfaction, for it is probable that I get more pleasure out of them than their rightful owners, when these ask me to lunch. To sit down to a meal about which one knows nothing beforehand, which one has not been seeing, smelling and tasting through various unattractive stages for the past two hours, is a form of bliss as rare as it is delicious—a bliss peculiar to this age, something at last quite new to the connoisseur of blisses.

It is true that I soon know exactly what everything is made of—not only from my own observation quickened by so much bitter experience that few casseroles can now enchant me with a mystery, but from the eager information of my hostess, who though she has not prepared the meal herself has had either to hoard or to hunt the material for it. Nevertheless there is still a large, delightful unexpectedness about it all, for I do not know exactly what is coming next and what exactly it will taste like. Besides, my hostess' range of materials is probably different from my own; perhaps she keeps a pig or someone has sent her a tin of smoked turkey from America.

Certainly for the country dweller, who cannot refresh herself with unknown food at a restaurant, an invitation to a meal in another woman's house is a treat whose value has increased some hundred per cent on the prewar figure. It is much better that this woman should have a cook, otherwise one has uneasy thoughts about all the labor she has been involved in by one's entertainment and I still do not know if the average hostess would rather her guest did or did not help with the washing up. But unfortunately women who have cooks are confronted with a problem which is bound to curtail the number of invitations they can issue and from which their cookless sisters are free.

The cook must be propitiated. Doubtless good cooks

have always had to be propitiated, but now the treatment must be extended to any sort of cook. "Oh, Sheila, do praise the thing that's coming next—it's a rabbit stew, a specialty of hers—at least she thinks it is—so do say it's nice, even if it isn't, which I'm afraid it won't be." Then there is the nervous rush to table directly Cook has rung the bell—for though there may still here and there be cooks there are broadly speaking no parlormaids to say in an indifferent voice—"Luncheon is served." There is also the dread of sitting too long over the meal, "because Cook wants to get washed up." And besides these openly expressed terrors there are those which one suspects are lurking at the back of the hostess' mind—memories of Cook's stark refusal to make a vanilla soufflé "because it's too much trouble" and her indignant protest at there being a visitor at all.

I am old enough to remember the days when people who wished to be thought well-bred never spoke about servants, because these were so commonplace a fact of life as to be unworthy of discussion. Now I find that people who have servants can talk of nobody else, and the people who have no servants can talk of nothing else, so either as a nation we have forfeited our last claims to good breeding or else—as I suspect—there was never anything particularly well-bred in ignoring the existence of so indispensable a section of the community.

When I was a girl life without servants was almost unknown except by those who were themselves of the servant class. Tradesmen, small shopkeepers, small farmers, all kept a maid or two. How well and how warmly I remember Emily, the maid at Platnix Farm, where my sister and I spent idyllic summer weeks when we were children. She had bare red arms and a mottled red face and she used to kill "wopses" with her thumb; but she wore a lace cap for all that.

My mother kept three maids besides our nurse—indeed, when I was very young there was also a nursemaid who one day fell downstairs—giving me my first taste of what the movie posters call "dramatic dynamite."

Only in a street newly blitzed have I ever felt since the full stifle of that horror and excitement which made my heart race as I was carried over the ruins of our nursery tea set.

Besides the nursery staff we had a cook, a house-parlormaid and a housemaid. I do not suppose that anyone today in my father's position would keep more than two maids, or indeed than one. But in keeping three he was doing no more—and as a doctor with a doorbell in constant agitation he might have done more —than anyone else in the street. In Arabella's house there also were three maids, and in every other house from No. 1 upwards to the top of the hill.

Forty-six houses . . . one hundred and thirty-eight maids in white caps and white aprons, pink dresses in the morning and black dresses in the afternoon . . . one hundred and thirty-eight maids, sleeping in basement bedrooms, eating in basement kitchens, carrying meals up basement stairs—up other stairs as well, for we had all our meals carried up to the nursery—carrying hot water to each bedroom four times a day, carrying coals for half a dozen scuttles, lighting and making up half a dozen fires, cleaning and black-leading half a dozen grates, sweeping carpets on their knees with dustpans and brushes, scrubbing floors, polishing furniture and "brasses" with polish they had to make themselves, light-ing the gas in every room and passage when darkness fell, besides all the business of cooking and waiting at meals and washing up afterwards. . . . No, I do not think we were overstaffed.

The house had been built in 1885, and when my par-ents took possession of it as its first tenants it was re-garded as a very latest expression of modernity and domestic enlightenment. It had, for one thing, a "house-maid's cupboard" halfway up the second flight of stairs, a sensational improvement on those houses where no water at all was laid on above the basement. We had a bathroom, too, and there was a cloakroom with hot and cold water taps on the ground floor. Gas was laid on throughout the house and there was a telephone. Nothing could be more up-to-date.

It was also considered an advantage that our "area" did not make a complete cavern of the basement, but blocked only about two-thirds of the window space. Indeed, in latter days, when maids were scarce, my mother used hopefully to call it a "semibasement." Certainly the kitchen, which faced almost due south, was a hot and sunny room. Cooking was done on a monstrous range which devoured a ton of coal every ten days or so, and was also supposed to heat the water; though as some rule of its construction forbade its doing this at the same time as its normal duties, there existed a perpetual state of conflict between meals and baths—the latter having sometimes to be taken at the most unusual hours.

In the basement, besides the kitchen, there was a huge scullery also equipped with a coal range but incapable of heating any water. There was also a pantry, with another sink, to which slugs from the garden had, most horridly, some secret mode of entrance. The servants' bedroom was in the front, overlooked from the doorstep and entirely sunless; and still there was room on the same floor for a lavatory (of the same ponderous construction as the one upstairs, but left unpainted just to show it was meant for servants), a vast and extremely good wine cellar (the only really well-planned room in the house but never containing anything more worthy of it than a few bottles of Australian Burgundy), a coal cellar housing six tons of coal and a storeroom which would have been appropriate had we lived in the wilds of the prairie instead of on the edge of a thriving seaside resort where the tradesmen called every day.

From this basement ascended a flight of uncarpeted wooden stairs, or rather two flights meeting on a landing lit by three sash windows and boasting a second back door from which one crossed the area on a viaduct with iron railings. At the top of the stairs was the main hall, soaring past two more flights (similar in construction to the first, except that they were varnished and carpeted), six enormous stained-glass windows, and two landings each as big as a double bedroom, till at last it came to the roof where—so vast, so sidereal, was the impression of space it managed to convey—you almost felt surprised that it should end in a ceiling instead of clouds.

For what purpose the unknown architect had designed this hall I cannot imagine. It was larger than the drawing room, but I do not think he meant it to be used except as a passage, for it contained no arrangements for heating—not even the smallest fireplace or any corner where it would be possible to fix a stove or a radiator. For light it depended on a single fishtail gas burner, held aloft by a bronze warrior on the first banister at the foot of the stairs. On a cold winter's night, with the darkness staring in through its six big rattling windows, I can think of no more dreary spot. Moira and I never played in it—preferring the less austere and drafty "lobby" between it and the front door, where stood a forest of sticks and umbrellas and where we conducted, amid many quarrels as to rite and precedence, Divine Service for our dolls every Sunday.

In the hall, however, was one really fascinating object and that was the telephone. I have been criticized for allowing the two children in *The Children's Summer*, a book of quasi-reminiscences, to use the telephone in their games. It was contended that children of that period would not have heard of the telephone, except perhaps as a distant invention. All I can say is that either I am not so ancient as my critic thinks or the telephone is not so modern. I suspect the latter, for the common tendency is to imagine various inventions and discoveries as much more recent than they actually are. Not only the telephone but electric light, the phonograph, and a spotty sort of "moving picture" were all in existence during my childhood, though only the first was really familiar.

Telephoning in those days, however, was not the same as it is now. No one would have picked up the receiver to spend a few minutes in comfortable chat with a friend. First you vigorously turned a handle to ring the bell and shouted: "Exchange! Exchange! Can you hear me?" Then followed a long series of "Are you there's?" before any real business could begin. Moira and I quite naturally were not allowed to touch the marvel; nor indeed could we have done so, for its ungainly bunch of boxes, wires and bells was set high out of our reach. But the shouts it necessitated could be heard all over the house, and in our nursery we would ring up tradesmen for our dolls in echo of our mother's frantic cries in the hall—"Is that Dengate—Dengate in the London Road? —Have you any tomatoes this morning?—no, tomatoes —I said tomatoes, not potatoes—no, not potatoes," and so on.

By the time I had grown from childhood to womanhood in that house, the little stock of "modern improvements" with which it and I had started life were hopelessly old-fashioned. Most people now had the telephone, nearly everyone had electric light and only a very few besides ourselves had not supplanted their coal-devouring kitchen ranges by gas cookers. It is true that we now had incandescent gas instead of fishtail burners and (which most people had not) a second bathroom. But when the end of the first World War brought us our first taste of real, genuine, unavoidable "servant trouble" it found us little better equipped for meeting it than we should have been in 1896.

My parents made many sacrifices, but they were nearly eighty years old and could not be expected to start a new life in which their early tea did not arrive at seven every morning. To make this happen it was necessary for their daughters to rise at five, for we had nothing to boil the kettle on but the kitchen range, which totally refused to respond to amateurs. One professional cook after another had lit it in a trice, but neither Moira nor I could do anything with it at all, and to my half-sister's efforts it responded only after hours of struggle, in the course of which she came to look less like a cook than a sweep.

·[22]·

Finally I lost patience and walked out to buy at my own expense an oilstove of almost volcanic activity, which boiled the early teakettle in five minutes. This was for some reason considered a low defeatist act, as was also my purchase of a carpet sweeper to supersede the dustpan and brush. The idea still existed in my family that laborsaving appliances were bound either to be destructive or grossly inferior in effect to the human efforts they relieved.

That idea still survives among conservative people, such as certain inhabitants of this part of Sussex, whom I have found, though they live under sixty miles from London, more determined than the Orkneys in their resistance to modern life. It was only with the greatest difficulty that I was able to persuade Mrs. Boorman, my excellent village "help" to use the electric cooker instead of the ancient and treacherous oilstove we keep for emergencies. Her daughter, too, a young woman of twenty-five, despises not only the carpet sweeper that shocked my Victorian parents, but the dustpan and brush they approved of—at least she thinks it necessary to follow up its use by smoothing every inch of the carpet with the palm of her hand.

6.

THE REAL QUESTION, OF COURSE, IS WHETHER YOU choose to make housework your main business or regard it as only a necessary job to be done in the intervals of your real work. Hitherto in this country, we have inclined to the former point of view—even at the end of six years of total war I am continually meeting women who are slaves to their houses and leave themselves entirely without energy if not without time for any wider interests. As a result we are years behind the housewives of America and Australia, who insist that their homes shall be so designed and organized that they can take their chosen part in life without neglecting them.

One reason for this no doubt, is that up till quite recently those women who had any power to change things had no wish because they had no need to do so; there were too many others to do the work for them. But this last war has surely dragged out of their indifference such of these as remained unshifted by the one before. A few years of struggling in their own ill-planned, ill-equipped kitchens, of coping with all their muddled arrangements for lighting and heating, with useless furniture and ornaments, dust traps and waste spaces, must surely have implanted in their minds a desire for better things. Shortly before the war I met a householder—a man, let me hasten to say—who declared that no tap in his house should ever be rustproof "because it made the servants lazy." I have a strong feeling that he may since then have changed his mind.

As for the working-class housewife, in country districts she had been at least partly shaken out of her conservatism by the necessity for combining housework with an outside job. When she comes home after a long day's toil in the fields or in some little local factory she cannot but look askance at her coal grate with its old-fashioned bars, at her "duck's nest" cooking stove that cannot produce the simplest hot meal in less than an hour, or the oilstove that has to be constantly trimmed and cleaned to function properly. She may even resent having to pump water from the well and decide not to oppose tooth and claw the next scheme (should there ever be one) for introducing a main water supply.

In towns the working-class woman is less conservative and also a little better off. She has at least "main" services of everything. But her home is not otherwise likely to be much more convenient than the average country cottage. It is both too large and too small—too large in the work it makes and too small in the accommodation it provides. In the town as in the country, most small houses are labor-making and awkward to live in; they have been allowed to slide out of repair and could now be rehabilitated only at a cost little less than the cost of rebuilding.

There are some large houses too in this category—houses like my old home, designed for a nursery full of children and a basement full of servants. Most of them have been turned more or less convincingly into flats, but a few remain in their Victorian wholeness—haunted as a rule by elderly survivors of the family, who live among familiar objects in familiar rooms a life as changed, as lonely and as helpless as a ghost's.

What are we going to do about all this? Our enemies have helped us toward a solution by knocking down a great deal of our unmanageable property. There is no political escape from a huge program of construction and reconstruction. Already, as I write, houses are being planned to bridge the inevitable gap between the nation's return to family life and the establishment of that life in homes where it can properly and permanently be carried on.

These houses are well imagined, in that they have many laborsaving improvements almost unknown in the average working-class home before the war. They are ill imagined, in that the designers of many of them do not seem to be really acquainted with the homelife of those for whom they are intended. They would do very well as the week-end bungalows of a leisured class, but for daily working life they are too small—not only in the number of rooms provided but in actual cubic space. The kitchen, especially, is too small to cook in for a family, and worse—it is too small for the family to eat in; which is a real drawback in circles where the parlor is needed for courting couples or for children doing homework.

But I have said, and I hope it is true, that these houses are only to bridge a gap. They are a this-war version of the last war outcrop of converted huts and henhouses in which our heroes camped comfortlessly until the building societies were able to put a better type of home within their reach. As such they certainly show a very great improvement in the national conscience, and even if as cramped and hideous as at first glance some of them appear, they are infinitely better than dwellings I have seen rise in past years among the Sussex woods—crazy shacks (I knew one built partly of disused stage scenery) which did not even offer adequate protection against the weather, let alone the amenities of civilized life.

The postwar house will not fail on the amenities—unless you catalogue privacy, quiet and space as such; on the contrary it should raise a hundred per cent the British housewife's standard of household equipment. Her kitchen panel of sink, stove, icebox and vegetable cupboard will promote her ideas to transatlantic levels, and she will certainly insist that no future house shall be built without at least the same amount of laborsaving installation. This should compel the owners of older property to bring it up to date in the same way, especially if these improvements are widely manufactured and easily installed. So I see the curtain rising on a nation of housewives of all classes equally endowed with leisure. Some of them have forgotten during the war what leisure is like—if they ever knew—and what women are to do with their leisure seems likely to be one of the female problems of the postwar world.

7.

IT IS NOT A NEW SITUATION. WOMEN'S LEISURE HAS BEEN a problem since the eighteenth century first allowed her to enjoy it. Until then her life—unless she was a very great lady indeed—had been absorbed in the business of living. Her household, even with the crowd of servants she employed, took up nearly all her thought and time. For everything had to be done at home—not only cooking and sewing and washing, but brewing, spinning and weaving, the making of soap and candles, of medicines, of beauty preparations. The household was entirely independent and self-contained.

Gradually these conditions relaxed, owing to the delegation of much of the work to an outer ring of tradesmen. By the end of the eighteenth century not only were materials for clothing to be bought in warehouses but they could be made up by tailors and seamstresses outside the home. Soap and candles too were to be found in the village shop, the laundry went to the washerwoman and the apothecary provided his medicines. As a result the lady of the house—encouraged by the spread of the undemocratic outlook which preceded the industrial revolution—was able to withdraw from the circle of her women and maids, leaving them to do the work of the house without her.

We can see this change of outlook as well as of custom reflected in Jane Austen's novels. In *Pride and Prejudice* Mrs. Bennet, a stupid, vulgar woman, is offended instead of complimented when Mr. Collins asks at dinner to which of his fair cousins the excellence of the cookery is due, and tells him "with some asperity that they were very well able to keep a good cook and that her daughters had nothing to do in the kitchen." She also despises her neighbor's daughter Charlotte Lucas for "being wanted about the mince pies. . . . For my part I always keep servants that can do their own work; *my* daughters are brought up differently." Though Jane Austen obviously does not approve of Mrs. Bennet, she treats her own literary daughters in much the same way. None of them is ever seen in the kitchen. Even Mrs. Price in *Mansfield Park* seems never to have gone to the assistance of her overworked and incompetent Rebecca. The lady of the house, be it large or small, is firmly settled in the drawing room.

This does not mean that she was idle. Idleness is a vice which this author never fails to scourge, and those characters who indulge in it are unfailingly held up to scorn. The more estimable majority filled their leisure with a mass of undertakings—sewing, of course, and embroidery and netting, but also with drawing, painting, singing, the pianoforte and the harp. A formidable range of "accomplishments" was taught in fashionable schools for the sole purpose of filling up these yawning gaps of leisure.

The first thing one notices is the extreme unproductiveness of most of the young ladies' employment. Sewing was useful to them and to their poorer neighbors, but the rest was mere time filling, as a rule. The necessity to play or sing or paint or draw came not from within but from without, and Jane Austen herself makes no pretense that many of her characters' performances were worth while. Some, no doubt, were able to fill the need for entertainment necessarily felt by those who lived in the country, far from theaters and concert halls, in days when music like everything else must be handmade. "I know of no greater pleasure," says Mr. Knightley in *Emma*, "than to sit by the fire listening to two such young lady performers as we had last night." Jane Fairfax, of course, was highly trained and talented, and Emma also gifted in a lesser degree; but I am very doubtful as to the real quality of Marianne Dashwood, Georgiana Darcey, Elizabeth Bennet and the two Miss Bertrams, and think it probable that in these days their families would prefer the radio.

By the end of the next century the whole system was coming into ridicule. It is true that when I was at school all but a few eccentrics learned the piano, and my parents experienced some doubts and some criticism when they stopped Moira's music lessons on the discovery that she could not recognize "God Save the Queen" unless the audience stood up. But we were no longer expected (as my mother was) to embellish the drawing room with our painted china and water-color sketches. Nor, unfortunately, were we ever taught to sew. I was at school from 1896 to 1904, but no one—either at home or at school—seemed to think sewing a necessary part of my education. As a result at the present day I can scarcely thread a needle, and am in the grotesque and humiliating position of having to ask my husband to sew on my buttons for me if I do not want them to come off again at once.

Women and girls in those days still had sacks of leisure, for houses were well staffed and housework not even to be thought of by the young ladies in the drawing room. They filled these sacks partly with elaborate social activities such as leaving cards, paying calls, being "at home" to visitors, going out to tea, organizing balls and charity concerts—partly with desultory efforts to improve their minds by reading and attending university extension lectures—partly by experimental good works such as Sunday school teaching, district visiting, or even "slumming."

I can remember it all very well, though I took no part in it, having saved myself from the petty wear and tear of such a life by having a novel published almost directly I left school. I was an author, a real, professional, paid author, so did not have to search for occupation. When I was not actually writing, I was walking, cycling or riding in the country—in the fields, lanes and villages where my heart and my work both were set.

Then the first World War came and leisure disappeared, never fully to return, for the servants never came back—at least not in their former numbers. Women were once more to be seen in their kitchens and showed some anxiety that their daughters should not spend years in expensive schools without learning to cook and sew. And thus the last war found us.

I do not expect it to leave us as it found us, nor as what it has made us—centaurs, half worker, half housewife, feeling that a paradise of rest and freedom would be open if we had only one job to do. For most of us, I expect, the outside job will be the job to go. But I do not think that many of us will want to return whole time to our kitchens, any more than to our whole-time drawing rooms. No doubt we shall still spend a certain number of hours in both, but we shall want to be able to walk in and out of them as we please.

We do not expect to win this freedom by paying other women to do our work, but by paying for ideas and appliances that will achieve the same result. We look for our leisure no longer to Mary Jane with her mop and broom but to some back-room boy with his blueprints. I do not see why such a change should disturb the integrity or even the beauty of our homes. There are domestic purists still, no doubt, just as there were in my mother's day; but I have no more sympathy with their nineteenth century ideals than I have with the rural purists' ideal of a return to the Middle Ages.

But the main problem is still unsolved. What are we to do with this new leisure?—almost certainly not what our grandmothers did. Music can now be had in every home by turning a knob, painted mats can be bought at the sixpenny store, and those of us who still like to hang pictures on our walls would probably rather leave them bare than adorn them with the exhibits of an Elinor Dashwood or an Emma Woodhouse.

We shall still have to find another outlet—stuffing, rather. Why is it that women's leisure is so much bigger a problem than men's? Men do not have to be told what to do with their spare time. They seem to have the choice of every satisfying recreation, from a scientific hobby to leaning against a gatepost. Perhaps the reason is that the average housewife had had in the past so little leisure that she has never attempted to fill it with anything but rest. Having cleaned the house, cooked the meals, looked after the children and spent the evening hour of relaxation in darning and mending, she can think of no finer recreation than sleep.

As for her wealthier sister, she is in many cases inhibited by that moral approach which well-bred women often bring to matters indifferent. It may be a sign of a guilty conscience. Certainly the most striking instance of it I have seen was in a family of ladies whose lives must have been almost entirely useless. They had not married, they had no jobs, their house was well staffed by competent servants. But they prided themselves on never being idle for a single moment. When waiting for a meal to be served they were busy with the sewing and knitting in their laps under the table, when they went for a picnic they legitimized the indulgence by sitting down on the grass to write letters, and every day they read from an improving book for exactly ten minutes by the clock. It takes a woman of the leisured class to see a moral duty in constant activity, and as a result many of them fall into a nervous habit of mind which makes rest only an irritation.

This complicates a problem which in this country has never been truly urgent until now. In America it has already been solved on lines which probably would not settle much over here. For many years the servantless American housewife has had nearly as much free time as the lady in the Victorian drawing room, and has been convinced, on the whole, of the necessity of filling it in a worthy rather than a frivolous manner.

I do not ignore the fact that the more equal numbers of men and women in the United States give the American woman a hold on jobs that in this country have been jealously clutched by men. A far greater proportion of women there than here go out to work, and use their emancipation from household slavery to establish themselves as independent wage earners. But even in America a large number of women, especially those no longer young, do not have jobs. How, then, do they fill their leisure?

I realized one method when I appeared on my first lecture platform in New York. The time was eleven o'clock in the morning—a discouraging hour and one at which in England it would have been virtually impossible to collect an audience at all. Yet I found the huge auditorium crowded, packed from wall to wall, almost entirely by women.

They certainly were not women of the working classes, but in this country even the middle-class housewife as a rule is housebound on Monday mornings. There is her laundry to count and send out, her shopping to do, a dozen little odd things to set in order after the relaxation of the weekend. If she were to go to a lecture at all it would be in the slack time of the afternoon, or in the evening when the business of the day is done.

But there those American women sat in their serried rows, having presumably, already at this early hour, dismissed the morning's cares and chores. After a light, easily cooked breakfast of coffee and corn-flakes they would have seen their husbands go off to work, and with electric cleaners, polishers and dishwashers have set their apartments to rights. Luncheon they would take at their clubs or at a drugstore. There were many hours still to run before they need be home again to prepare the evening meal. What they had to think of now was the most agreeable way, most profitable way of filling those hours; and they chose to fill at least one of them by improving their minds at a lecture.

It is an admirable idea, but unfortunately it stops far short of realization. For I am convinced that the average lecture which the American woman attends is about as likely to improve her mind as painting mats. I found when I was in the United States that the appetite for these lectures was insatiable, that some women were capable of attending a lecture a day, and that the price of admission was often as much as we should pay in England for a stall at the theater. In fact the lecture was "for entertainment only."

At first, misled by such names as "The Literary and Philosophical Society" and "The Academy of Arts and Sciences" I imagined that something of the nature expected by the larger London literary societies was required. But I soon found out that what my audience really wanted was a sort of prolonged after-dinner speech, delivered in much the same style as those painful wisecracking commentaries that accompany transatlantic newsreels. It took me a long time to learn this new technique; indeed I do not think that I ever mastered it. Perhaps I had behind me too many years of lecturing to English and—most serious of all—Scottish audiences to be able to make a successful soufflé of what I had always regarded as solid fare.

Most responsible lecture societies in this country take it as a matter of course when the lecturer reads a paper instead of delivering an improvised speech. In fact I have had on at least one occasion to apologize for speaking extemporally, and, though forgiven, felt reproached when later on the chairman referred automatically to my speech as my "paper." But I shall not easily forget the trouble there was when my personal idiosyncrasy of speaking in paragraphs aroused in the bosoms of a certain Brooklyn audience the suspicion that I had read my lecture.

The circumstance that made the biggest impression on my memory was the behavior of the lecture agency. It wrote to remonstrate, but it did not write to *me*; it wrote to my husband. Having laid before him the audience's point of view, it asked him, "if a favorable opportunity should arise," to persuade me to change my methods. But they hastened to add that if no favorable opportunity arose they would not expect him to open the subject. Needless to say this letter interested me far more as a wife than as a lecturer. It suggested so many fascinating queries as to conjugal life in the United States (or possibly only in the lecture agency) that the immediate aspects of the situation became comparatively dim.

I am sure that no lecture society in this country would feel insulted if a lecture were read to them. A "paper" is indeed a respectful gesture to the audience. It guarantees the integrity of the subject in a way no improvisation can do. It proclaims a careful, indeed laborious, preparation and safeguards accurate reporting. But, of course, unless read by a genius or a professional actor, it is not so entertaining. British audiences do not as a rule go to lectures to be entertained. They go more or less as students, to acquire information. Therefore very few of them go.

In this matter they are perhaps more European than Anglo-Saxon. We British do not yet on a large scale expect to have instruction combined with entertainment. But I am doubtful as to how long, in a world where leadership seems more and more likely to pass from the old, mature, weary nations to the young, eager and inexperienced, we shall be able to maintain this fastidiousness. The Anglo-Saxon is on the whole a frothy creature, and giddily fond of surfaces. The education we give to our children is a frail, tittupy thing compared with that dispensed on the Continent. The years that pass seem to take us further and further from our own depths, to put us more and more in danger of superficialities and oversimplifications, to promise minds relaxed rather than fortified by the increasing wealth of leisure.

But what, the reader may now well ask, do I hope that women will do with their leisure? Well, anything except paint mats. For mats are surfaces in extreme, surfaces on a surface, without depth, roots or attachment to what is beneath. It does not matter how many are painted or how wide an expanse they cover, they are still only on the top and can be swept away by any draft or commotion. The widening of women's interests and occupations will only spread the surfaces of life more thinly if there are no depths to call upon, no foundations with which the superstructure is continuous.

Baron von Hugel when directing an adult niece's religious education urged her to lay the foundations of a Christian life in the knowledge of Greek and Latin philosophy, history, poetry, and numismatics as well as in patristic and scholastic theology. He urged her, too, to "cultivate more carefully and lovingly the interests, the activities that are not directly religious." He was determined that her religion should not be a mat, sliding on the surface of things without any real connection with them, a mat which might cause even her careful-stepping soul to slip. "How thin and abstract, or how strained and unattractive, the religion of most women becomes, owing to their elimination of religion's materials!"

For heaven's sake let us not widen women's interests without deepening them. This lack of depth is apparent now in almost every aspect of our country's life, and I see it increasing with the greater facilities for leisure and recreation that the future will bring to most of us, particularly to women.

I see before us, if we are not careful, a new era of the half-baked—half-baked political theories, half-baked social remedies, half-baked literary and artistic fashions, half-baked religions and half-baked sciences and philosophies. For the tendency of our thought is still to produce surfaces—crisp, golden surfaces (for we are back in the kitchen now with a new metaphor), but unfortunately only the appetizing crust of a raw, uncooked mess, which in the end will give us all indigestion.

If this is all we can do with our new opportunities we should be better off without them, better off at the old grind, better off taking a different sort of risk and becoming hard-boiled from struggle and overwork. To be hard-boiled may be a limiting, desiccating process, but at least it is not unwholesome—we shall do better with a hard-boiled life than a half-baked one. If the future should compel a choice, I, for one, should prefer the first. But I cannot suppress a foreboding that the world of peace and plenty to which we look forward is capable, unlike the kitchen stove, of producing a dyspeptic combination of both.

Part II

Episodic

_____

1.

EARLY IN THE WAR I REALIZED THAT I OUGHT TO LEARN to cook. There had been no signs of urgency—nothing happened to suggest the call-up of women which was later to strip so many kitchens of their motive power. The idea was prompted less by apprehensions of the future than memories of the past. I remembered the devastation caused by the last war in my mother's home and I did not want to be caught unprepared by any later stages of this.

Cooking was my main anxiety, partly because I had no experience of it—whereas I had done my fair if clumsy share of sweeping, dusting and bedmaking—and partly because I knew that for ordinary housework I had a reservoir of local talent to draw from, whereas the local cooks had inspired me only with dread of their tender mercies.

Besides, though I had not actually practiced the art, I was deeply interested in it and had a passable knowledge of its theory. Ever since I became a housekeeper in my own right I had been careful to engage good cooks and had enjoyed planning meals, trying new ideas, introducing new recipes and new kinds of things to eat. I could not bear the thought of being left in inexpert hands or floundering helplessly by myself through a painful system of trial and error.

I imagined, like most people who have not tried it,

that cooking is much more difficult than it actually is. This belief is encouraged by professional cooks, who naturally make the best of their job and like to give the impression that it involves the maximum of experience and inspiration. It has also in my case been encouraged by their failures. In my mother's house we had such a long succession of incompetent professionals that I was led to believe that the odds must be heavily against them. Otherwise it would seem incredible that they should be able to earn their living as cooks. Cooking must be full of snares and snags or no one would pay a salary to such blunderers.

This idea was borne out by meals in the houses of my friends. As a girl I cannot remember a single home where the food was better than in ours, but several in which it was even worse. I can remember soggy suet rolls, lumpy sago puddings, rhubarb sticks so hard they could be snapped and stewed gooseberries so sour that my gums recede at the bare recollection. I can remember too my dread of these feasts. At home if anything especially disgusted me I was allowed to substitute bread and butter or a slice of toast. But in friends' houses one had to be polite and swallow what was on one's plate and avoid retching.

Even at Arabella's we never had anything "nice," as we had for tea. Why did we fare so badly? Was it the standard of our time or of our town?—or just of our own little circle, too poor to pay expensive cooks, too genteel for the lady of the house to concern herself actively in the kitchen? Certainly if a cook came to us from our friends she could be relied on to be no better than the one who was leaving us. "She can't do more than roast or boil" is a reference stamped on my memory—partly by the fact that "She" could do neither. It was not till I was grown-up and had friends in London that I knew that a well-cooked, palatable meal could be served in a private house.

When I came to employ a cook of my own there was a higher standard, but still this mysterious sense of frustration. For several years I had a cook so excellent in her public performances that a friend who was "returning our cutlet" at the Café Royal told me afterwards that he had urged the headwaiter to produce something very special as we had given him the best dinner he had ever eaten in a private house. Yet the cook who had so marvelously entertained him could not make an ordinary omelet. She could make an *omelette surprise*, but not an *omelette aux fines herbes* in either the French or the English style. It always turned mysteriously to leather. Neither could she make soup; I used to buy my soup in bottles from Fortnum and Mason. Nor could she make any sort of hot soufflé, though she was a supreme artist at every sort of cold mousse. It was a surprise to me later on when I had much homelier cooks who could do these things, and the biggest surprise of all was when I found I could do them myself.

I have never made—nor do I suppose that I shall ever make an *omelette surprise*; but I have made at the first attempt a perfectly good hot cheese soufflé and if I find anything easier than making an omelet it is making soup. What did she do to obstruct herself in these simple things? The cause of a cook's failures is just as interesting as the cause of her successes. Yet somehow one never dares to vary the familiar question and ask—"Oh, Cook, do please tell me exactly what you did to make that omelet—soufflé—soup—whatever it was—so revolting?"

2.

I PIGEONHOLED THE IDEA OF LEARNING TO COOK UNTIL the war was some months old. I was in no immediate hurry, having an excellent cook whom I also liked very much as a human being. Besides, my house was full of evacuees, which would have complicated past all endurance my start in the kitchen.

It is like looking back into another war to remember that this battered corner of England was once a reception area, with its population nearly doubled by refugees from more dangerous parts, and that our derelict coast towns spent their first war Christmas on a boom, crowded with evacuees, military trainees and visitors to both.

But this has been a war of phases—unlike the one before which I remember as a monotony only occasionally relieved by some change of catastrophe, such as the sinking of the "Lusitania" or the death of Kitchener. This war started, as everybody knows, as a "phony" war. The invasion of Poland by Germany was too remote to compete in popular interest with the invasion of the English countryside by the inhabitants of London and the big towns. For several months we lived very much as in peacetime, except that certain familiar faces had gone and many unfamiliar ones came in their stead.

Then came a new phase—some weeks of indignation and foreboding while Germany overran Norway, the Netherlands and finally France. The fall of France left us shocked and bewildered to face the Battle of Britain and its dragon-tail of the Blitz. The Blitz ended suddenly when Hitler marched on Russia, but by this time we were going through too many shortages and struggles at home to slide back into the "phony" stage. There was also the North African campaign to keep us proud and alert. Besides, Hitler was not having the fun in Russia he had had in Poland, and after a time we began to think that once again—as when he failed to invade this disarmed country after Dunkirk—we were to profit from his mistakes.

A phase peculiar to this part of England was the "tip and run" blitz—no capital letter this time—on small, rather shabby areas of the east and southeast coasts, when the mighty Luftwaffe seemed to think it strategically worth while to concentrate on killing old ladies and smashing seaside lodginghouses. This ended as soon as the resorts concerned had been provided with adequate means of defense. Then came our own punch back and a totally new aspect of war, as the Allies moved to the offensive. Four years after the fall of France, British and American troops landed in Normandy and we began to see the end.

But we were still for some time to be on the defensive in Kent and Sussex, as the flying bombs came over from what is known to our cottage neighbors as the Palais de Calais, to be showered by our own guns and planes on our own fields and farms and villages. Having started the war as a reception area we were now to become an evacuation area and see our own women and children sent away toward the uncertain hospitality that we ourselves had dispensed in the past.

No doubt some scheme of evacuation was necessary, both at this time and at the beginning of the war, but I shall never understand why, with the long months the authorities had to prepare it, both earlier and later, the whole thing should have borne such heavy marks of improvisation, of a first hasty conception unrevised either by thought or by experience.

It seemed at almost every aspect to cut across some common human instinct. It undertook to separate husbands and wives for an indefinite period, and only a little less lightheartedly to separate mothers and children. It thrust town-bred people into remote countrysides where they were bored almost to panic—I know of one East End borough evacuated to a district where there was only one bus a week to the nearest town twelve miles away. It also ignored the national complex of the Englishman's Home, that tight little island which even his next-door neighbor invades at his peril. It expected him not only to open it to strangers at a price which did not pay for their keep, but it expected two women—one from the fields and the other from the slums—to agree in what can only rarely have approximated to King Solomon's idea of a wide house.

I know that nothing much better than this could have been done in 1938, when we country dwellers made our first bewildered preparations to receive the towns; but a year later, and certainly four years after that, even a government department might have devised a more workable plan. I note only two improvements in the later edition. Mothers whose children were all of school age were allowed to accompany them, and confirmed townspeople were evacuated to other towns. But we were still up against the system of private billeting, which made so much misery not only for the landlady but for the refugee, and we still paid a sum which was inadequate in 1939 and must in 1944 definitely have put the housekeeper out of pocket.

Surely the organization of camps and hostels would have been possible some time between Munich and D-Day—a period during the whole of which the danger was foreseen and proclaimed with many public warnings. Human beings are not yet so venal that they will pay an indefinite price for safety, nor yet, I fear, so self-sacrificing that they will cheerfully allow their lives and their homes, their incomes and their kitchen stoves to be disrupted by less fortunate strangers.

I do not think that at the beginning of the war our village was more inhospitable than other places—then or later. I know that we expected the worst. Rumor had prepared us for a vomit of squalor and unruliness, of ignorance and vermin—is not London famous in Sussex as the home of London Bugs? We had made preparations to delouse the strangers immediately on arrival. It was surprising therefore to see emerge from the first busses an orderly procession of schoolboys and schoolgirls wearing the uniform of a well-known technical school in South London. We forgot about the delousing and withdrew to our second line of welcome, which was, more hospitably, a meal of cake and tea.

A big elementary school followed—not so smart but perfectly clean; then came the mothers and under-fives —the most dreaded of all. I had not shared this dread and had offered to take out my quota entirely in mothers and children. We had been assessed at seven, and I felt unequal to coping with that number of restless small boys or homesick small girls, all of whom would have had to be washed, fed and clothed under my supervision if not actually by my hands.

But when we came to business we found it comparatively easy to dispose of the boys and girls. The cottagers were quite ready to take them and often gave them the kindest welcome, while one or two larger houses had accommodation both for them and for their teachers. But several of the mothers and babies were left like unsold turkeys on our hands at the end of a day of frantic exertion and persuasion. Families of six and eight and ten who refused to be separated were an insoluble problem in a village where homes are mostly small, and in the end a derelict rectory of vast proportions had to be taken for their accommodation.

As it happened, those who accepted this unpopular form of refugee, did not fare so badly, for at the end of the week nearly all of them had gone home. It is difficult to think how anyone could have seriously expected them to stay, unless London had been pounded to ruins on the first night of the war. They were worried and anxious about their husbands—that they would not be able to manage without them or that they would manage only too well. They were worried and anxious about their children in another woman's house, and about their own inhibitions in another woman's kitchen. "Use of kitchen" is a ticklish condition of tenancy, even when the lodger is paying a good sum for it, and I owe the peace in which my own evacuees lived with me for over three months very largely to the fact that I had an extra room which I was able to equip with a large oil cooking stove for their exclusive use.

They were also badly disillusioned in what was for many their first experience of the English countryside. For the chastisement of our village I might have collected their verdicts on the place—of which "mortuary" and "cemetery" were among the least offensive. It was a mystery to them how anyone could voluntarily live in such a hole, and when the bombs did not fall on London they fled back there from a silence and loneliness more terrifying than any blitz.

My own evacuees remained with me till Christmas, when the pretense was politely made and politely accepted that they were going home for the holidays. They did not dislike the country as much as some of the others, though we are over two miles from the village, and they realized that their children must thrive in the fresh air, with a garden to play in and all the free delights of fields and lanes. But I am sure they would not have stayed if they had had to share my small kitchen. Indeed I cannot think how we should have managed in those circumstances—which were, after all, the circumstances that ordinarily prevailed—for each one of my three mothers insisted on cooking separately for her family and each child was trained to believe that only Mother's cookery was fit to eat.

At first I had imagined that the mothers would cook by turns, but this notion was politely but firmly rejected at the very start.

"You see, my little boys would never eat anything that Mrs. Stevens cooks. They only eat what I do."

And the same went by Bill Stevens and Tessa Long.

As a result, the atmosphere of their living room can have been only a few degrees cooler than their oven, for the oilstove was always in a state of high eruption. Not only did each mother cook her own meals, but no mother and no child ever seemed to eat a cold one—no cold meat or pudding, no sardines even for supper. All three families walked every day to the village for their shopping, and consumed that same day everything they had bought. They never planned ahead or left the smallest scrap for next day's use. Their methods had a morbid fascination for my old cook.

"I said to them, 'I never in my life saw anyone cook so much as you'. I said 'you cook twice as much as I do, and *I'm paid for it.*'"

Those of course were days of plenty—no rations, no "points," the shops full of meat and bacon and all sorts of groceries. My evacuees were not short of money, for their husbands were all in good, if small, lines of business—one as a tailor, one as a hairdresser and one in the provision trade. They were anxious that their families should have every possible comfort in their exile.

They also seldom left them a weekend unvisited, even though the journey involved a twenty-five mile bicycle ride from the junction. At weekends I ceased to count heads—husbands, fathers, mothers, brothers, sisters sat all day in the oven living room and slept at night I knew not where. Certainly we all liked one another and when Christmas came parted the best of friends, my mothers having given their rooms a clean-out that included even the windows but excluded for some reason the floors. My real regret at their departure was regarded in the village as a morbid symptom.

3.

TO THE SECOND PHASE OF THE WAR BELONGS MY initiation as a cook. It was not strictly speaking an initiation, but rather a preparation, a postulancy to open the way to the novitiate. For I was not yet a cook in my own kitchen—only a student at a school of cookery.

The school was in the neighboring seaside town, and the time was June, 1940. Driving into the town one faced the dark curtain which the burning oil stores of the French ports had drawn across the sea—a curtain which one day was to blacken the whole sky. In the town itself one witnessed the shock and bewilderment of a place which for months had lived softly and safely as a popular refuge and now suddenly found itself in the front line. The more nervous and well-to-do of the inhabitants were already leaving, the shops were deserted, the hotels were closing, the schools evacuating, and the jolly Air Force cadets who for so long had splashed the streets and promenade with blue were being moved to a more favorable training ground. It was not a panic, not a flight, but a sort of surprised disruption.

Poor old town! Since that day you have suffered the fury of the Hun as much as any place in England and more than most. You have been threatened with invasion, tangled with barbed wire and barricaded with walls of brick and bottle glass, "banned" to visitors, stripped of your inhabitants; you have been used as a practice ground for Nazi bombers long before London knew the Blitz, for months when London was safe you have been battered by tip-and-run raiders, and then defended London with a mighty barrage which rocked and bounced your few lingering citizens and brought down the maimed fly-bombs on your already battered streets. You have had some two thousand alerts, and rumor says that when the robot menace came your exhausted siren blew its last warning and awaited the end of the war for the All Clear.

In this threatened borough my ignorance was dispelled to the extent of six cookery lessons. The teaching was practical—no time wasted in lectures and demonstrations but the experience gained of my own hands plunging into flour or slipping over raw meat, my own fingers burning on the stove, my own eyes watering over onion peel. What I had always known I needed to learn had been the *feel* of things, all the messy, sticky, slithery side of cooking. Till I had experienced that I knew that I was only a theorist, a *voyeuse*, lacking the elements of practice. I believe that only exceptional minds can learn from demonstration. Going into battle with the kitchen stove requires something more than rifle practice and bayonet drill in preparation—something like our modern battle schools, which are the result of the same discovery of the gulf that yawns between demonstration and experience.

By the time the Germans were in the Channel ports I had with my own pair of hands made *gnocchi à la romaine*, *bonne femme* soup and *sole Normande*, cooked spinach and cauliflower, roasted and stuffed a joint. I had snatched these **acquirements** as it were from under Hitler's nose and I was exceedingly proud of them.

In my defense it must be remembered that until then I had not even boiled an egg, and the boiling of an egg has always been considered the simplest, most completely foolproof process in the whole art of cookery. With this I cannot agree, for some abasing experiences have taught me that it requires just as much thought and judgment as anything else. I know know why professional cooks of otherwise good attainment so often failed to give me an egg boiled as I like it, with the yolk just set; and I no longer disbelieve the story once told me by an actor friend about a theatrical landlady who could serve a boiled egg raw at one end and burnt at the other.

In the first place it is easy to forget to look at the time when one puts the egg into the saucepan; in the next it is easy (at least to me) to forget about the egg altogether. Even professional cooks are apt to be a little cavalier about the clock. I once had a German cook who told me that in boiling eggs she always relied upon her intuition, and as a result we had Stalingrad for breakfast every morning.

Moreover, eggs do not all behave the same way in boiling water. My own have a tendency to explode with a loud report, which is due, no doubt, to some weakness in the shell caused by the poor hen's wartime diet and deficiency of oyster grit. This reaction frightens me so much that when I boil an egg with a doubtful-looking shell I leave the kitchen till the worst is over. All is not lost, however, when I return, for the boiling water hardens the emergent glair (that is the proper name for the "white"—I learned it from a crossword puzzle) and one's egg is still edible as long as one does not mind its being partly inside out.

Eggs that burst while boiling bring me back to the theme of war, for that has caused a great many objects in my vicinity to burst with very much louder noises than eggs or even than those paper bags which, blown up with the mocking breath of errand boys, used to cause me so much anguish as a child.

For as long as I can remember I have had a terror of noise. I cannot tell how or when it started, but my mother had it too, and added her example to hereditary by startled reactions to every untoward sound. On my first visit to the pantomime I was taken out before the final curtain, because it came down on a pony firing a pistol and my elders decided that this would fill me with panic and spoil an otherwise unblemished treat. Unfortunately the move was made too late, and the pistol went off before I had left the Pier Pavilion. My head still seems to hold that rolling crack of sound . . . but I cannot hook my neurosis—for with me it has reached the point of neurosis—to the shock of that moment, for it was probably already in situation. It is the case of the chicken and the egg—I do not know which came first.

Children's parties were a terror to me because of the crackers, and I enjoyed without qualm only those drab shows where they were not provided. If they were, I generally demanded to be taken from the room directly after tea, before the cracker pulling began. I must have been an appalling nuisance to my hosts—I have at least one humiliating picture of myself, sitting with the long-suffering adult who had escorted me from the feast, and making hypocritical face-saving conversation which she at last cut short by reading to me a story entitled "Charles: or the New Pink Frock."

Or was that a clock-chiming occasion? . . . For I used to ask to be taken away if I thought the clock was going to strike. The striking of a clock filled me with a desperate, morbid fear, and as a result I learned to read the time at an exceptionally early age. On arriving at an unknown house I would always start making polite remarks about the clock—how pretty it was! Did it strike? . . . No, unfortunately the chime was broken (Hurrah for an unspoilt afternoon) . . . or only the hour (well at least I've fifty minutes to go before misery begins) . . . or yes, and it chimes the quarters (do you

·[47]·

think I might go out into the garden?—or may I go up to the nursery?—or even, in extreme cases, may I go home?)

Fortunately, for myself and others, I have got over the clock-chiming, cracker-pulling complexes. But I am still terrified of guns and pistols, and never go willingly to a play if I know that there is anything of that sort to be expected. Before the last war I refused to see "An Englishman's Home," and before this war "Journey's End," entirely because of their explosive realism. And I still walk out of the kitchen if I think my boiling egg is going to pop.

By now I hope the reader's sympathies are roused. He realizes what I have been going through during the last five years. If I jump out of my clothes at the pop of a boiling egg, what did I do when a burst of machine-gun fire rattled over my head to be followed by the burst of a thousand-pound fly-bomb? How did I enjoy the hundreds of bombs that were dropped in my neighborhood during the Blitz and the Battle of Britain?

It was in connection with the latter that both my half-sisters separately inquired—"How are you liking the noise? For I shall never forget how you . . ."

What Thea would never forget was the ghastly occasion when taking me, in her kindness, for a picnic on donkey back, we found ourselves overtaking a young man carrying a gun. The lane led up from the village to the moor, where no doubt the young man hoped for a little sport. Certainly he could have no idea of firing his gun then and there in the lane. But nothing would convince me otherwise, and I burst into desperate screams. I yelled and howled for at least half a mile, till at last the sportsman turned round to ask what was the matter.

"I'm afraid it's your gun," said my crimson sister.

"My gun? But what?—why?—Is she frightened of my gun?"

"Yes. She thinks you're going to fire it."

"But I've no intention of doing so—here."

"No, of course not."

I was making such a noise that I could not hear a word they said. The mere fact of his standing still had swelled my screams to eldritch power. But here the donkey intervened—she disliked noise too, and there was too much of it on her back. She stood still, spread out her forelegs, and shook herself violently. The scene abruptly changed, and by the time I was once more in position the young man had disappeared—no doubt he had escaped through the nearest gate from the panic he had created. But my poor sister's blushes had almost become a dye.

My other sister recalls an equally humiliating occasion. She had taken Moira and me for a walk on the sea front—I can't think now how anyone ever took me out unless they were paid to do so. As we were on our way home some guns began to fire—no doubt in practice by the Rifle Volunteers, who were the only people in those days to make explosions in our parts. I burst into screams and Moira—though she was not naturally gun-shy—paid me the compliment of imitation. Off we went, blest pair of sirens, howling and wailing our way along the parade. Dulcie had seized a hand of each—she has told me since that she was afraid we would run away and hurl ourselves under the traffic—and this did not help matters, because in such an emergency, then, as now, I wanted to hold my ears. I could do this only with one hand and I fought in vain to possess myself of the other. Thus we staggered along, a spectacle of shame and anguish both adult and infantile, till finally a Bath-chair man intervened with his idea of comfort—"They won't hurt you, missy."

This intervention was for some reason so unspeakably horrible that it swallows up the rest of the episode in my memory, and probably now it would require mental analysis to drag it forth, though I'm sure my poor sister has only too clear a picture of how we reached home. "They won't hurt you, missy" . . . as if I thought they would! That Bath-chair man had not the rudiments of understanding as far as little Sheila's reactions to gun-fire were concerned. I did not think the guns would hurt me any more than I thought the crackers would hurt me, or the chiming clocks. It was the noise I was afraid of—the hateful, harmless noise—just as I was afraid of the patch on my father's dressing room ceiling, of his trouser-press and the places where the enamel had been chipped off the bath. I never thought those things could hurt me. They were just horrible and frightening in themselves.

In the last war I used to say that I did not mind the noise of air raids, because nobody ever told me "They won't hurt you." But I did not say the same in this. Indeed, the fact that the whole thing was, roughly speaking, designed to hurt me, gave it a sinister quality which was about the only horror lacking before. I sometimes found a doubtful comfort in the thought that the Hun would much rather hurt somebody else, that he would be acutely disappointed to know that he had wasted one of his expensive bombs on me. This idea did away with some of the personal side of the malevolence, but I do not recommend it for general consolation. In fact, I write these lines only on the assumption that by the time they are read the tyranny of noise and hate and danger will be over, and no one's fortitude will be even ever so little impoverished by the revelations of a poor wretch who has to endure being afraid of what no people in their senses are afraid of as well as what all people in their senses are.

4.

BUT I STILL HAVE NOT BEGUN TO COOK, THOUGH THE time is growing nearer, and in theory, at least, I am prepared. Actually it was the autumn of 1942 before I found myself a cook in literal fact. For two years I had been told by others and had also told myself that I should never be able to hold together the double business of cooking and writing and that it was better to put up with inefficient professionals than to muddle up a job I could do by attempting (and probably also muddling) theirs. "There's so much more in it than you realize," was the parrot cry of my friends, including past cooks. But when I came to doing the job I found, not more in it than I had expected, but very much less.

For one thing, I found that, being my own mistress, I could cook just as little as I chose and my first act was to abolish the convention of two main meals a day, which I had been forced to observe as long as I had maids living in the house. My husband's work as well as our joint preference had required our chief meal to be in the evening, but I have seldom known a professional cook or housemaid who did not insist on having hers at midday. She would gladly share ours in the evening too, but there must also be a midday dinner of at least two courses if she was not to consider herself as worse off than in a concentration camp. Equally difficult in wartime I had found her opposite—the type who with a virtuous air asserts "I never want anything myself but bread and butter or bread and cheese," and then proceeds to consume the entire household rations of both.

Before I took over the kitchen I had had for a time both these types in residence, for my old Nellie had gone. When invasion threatened the country she could not bear to be away from her sister and their little home in London, and the offer of a home with us for the sister was no solution, as obviously Hitler would come to Sussex before he came to Streatham. So she went off just in time for the London blitz.

It was not then too difficult to find a successor, though none to equal my old Nellie either at the cooking of a meal or the sharing of a joke. Things slowly got worse, until in the spring of 1942 I realized that Rosalind was eating all the meat, bacon and eggs and Elizabeth all the butter, margarine and cheese. You may say that I should have prevented them—kept the rations locked up and doled them out piecemeal (already no doubt they were blaming my meanness rather than the fortune of war for such restrictions as they were unable to escape). But from moral cowardice, if you like, I preferred to get rid of them altogether.

I have always loathed Victorian methods of mistrust —they seem to poison the very roots of the relationship between mistress and maid; and the fact that there obviously is a need for them only shows how fundamentally unsatisfactory under modern conditions is the whole of that relationship, how urgently in need of reform.

In ancient times servants were regarded and treated as junior members of the family (famulus—a name applying alike to servants and to sons); and when they ceased to be this they lived in a self-contained, self-sufficing world of their own. They were still employed in sufficient numbers to be safe from tyrannous suppression on one hand or loneliness on the other. It was not till a changed social system scattered them in twos and threes that we see the relationship between employer and employed becoming vitiated.

Jane Austen gives us in *Mansfield Park* one of the earliest instances of "servant trouble" in fiction. When Fanny Price goes to stay with her family in Portsmouth she finds her mother in a perpetual state of war with the "trollopy looking servant girl," and is shocked by the contrast between her ways and the ways of Mansfield Park. "What does my sister Bertram do for servants?" is a question that received and required no answer, for in the Bertrams' huge establishment the problem did not exist. It was the small household with its cramped associations that made trouble then as it does today.

No one is likely to employ as many servants at four pounds a week as they used to do at four pounds a year, so there is no chance of the big establishment returning, with its free and jolly company. I imagine that even the six-servant house, still existing precariously before the war, is a thing of the past and that houses that employ one or two resident maids will in future be exceptional.

I am not sorry, for I do not think that much can be done with the relationship between mistress and maid in the state to which time and abuses have brought it. It needs replanting—pulling up by the roots and replanting. Just as the days of the huge establishment, with its independent Second World, are gone, so too are the days of a fellow human being sharing our homes without sharing our lives, having all the work without any of the fun, responsibility without possession, leisure without liberty.

Instead, no doubt, we shall have a morning visitor, arriving from her hostel at the scheduled hour and reducing our house to order in the scheduled time before she goes on to do the same for someone else's. Possibly hours and salaries will be fixed by law, as they are in other trades. Possibly domestic service will become a department of the civil service. . . . I hope that some alternative scheme may be devised for those who live in the country out of reach of hostels, and that those will not be forgotten who are too old and helpless to have their requirements met by schedule.

The rest of us, of course, will have to manage for ourselves some twenty hours, at least, out of the twenty-four. The days of genteel idleness are over—the ghost of the Victorian lady who rang the bell when she dropped her handkerchief will gaze at us reproachfully, and not so much reproachful as indignant will be the gaze of that Victorian lady's cook. Never so completely will we lose caste as with such old-fashioned servants as still remain, embedded like fossils in prewar strata.

Personally I would rather do housework than office work, but I hope I shall not lose my present privilege of determining what kind of housework I shall do. I imagine that most women will exercise the right of selection, choosing the special work for which they feel themselves adapted and leaving the rest to the Home Helps or whatever they are called. A great many conventions will

·[53]·

have to be swept overboard and a number of new ways learned; but if all this coincides with a general improvement in housing—and in that term I include the houses of the rich as well as of the poor—the housewife's lot will not be altogether an unhappy one.

For three years now I have had visiting "dailies" only and I can bear witness that no arrangement has given more satisfaction to all concerned. This is a fair-sized house—specially designed to be run with the help of a resident married couple—and I should be sorry to find myself in it with no help at all. But it is a delight to have it to myself for the greater part of the day, to be independent, to enjoy real privacy and the freedom to be as eccentric as one sometimes feels. My "women," who live near, come and go as they please and divide up the work among themselves as suits them best. There are no worries about time off, no "That isn't my work, madam," no controversies about food and rationing, no inferiority complexes. They are living their own lives and I am living mine, which is what is so important and so pleasant for us all.

Matters, of course, have been made easier by the fact that I have chosen to do the cooking rather than the housework. Writing and cooking combine more smoothly than writing and sweeping or writing and bedmaking. I write in the morning and cook in the evening, so the two jobs are kept well apart. Breakfast is produced by Mrs. Sivyer, the morning "help," who then goes home and does not reappear. Queenie Boorman does all the housemaid's chores, and her mother comes in soon after seven to dish up and wash up our evening meal. Those intermittent jobs such as answering the doorbell or the telephone, which might otherwise have interfered with my literary work are settled by the simple act of placing myself out of earshot of both.

I could not have taken such evasive action with either sweeping or bedmaking, which was one of my reasons for turning cook. Another was the realization that though I could find in the neighboring cottages three pleasant, efficient women, who would do ordinary house-work much better than I, I should have been risking both my own and my husband's digestion had I exposed them to the rigors of Sussex *cuisine*.

One of the few drawbacks of this county is its lack of any characteristic school of cookery. It has no historic dishes or ways of eating, such as are the pride of other parts of England. Indeed, you will find a Sussex farm-house shamelessly advertising Devonshire teas, for un-like Devonshire, Sussex has no cream worth mentioning. The local strain of cattle are notoriously poor milkers and the coarse, rank grass that grows most easily on the Wealden clay is no help to the dairy.

Nor have we local cheeses, as in the west, or local cakes and pies as in the north. I have heard certain cakes, such as "lardy Johns" proclaimed as of Sussex origin, but they are to be found all over agricultural England and no doubt express the old-time laborer's idea of heaven in something really fat and filling. Of course there is South Down mutton, famous throughout the world; but our Sussex women have no proud ways of cooking it, for the reason that though the shepherd watched ceaselessly over his flock, he seldom if ever had a taste of their meat.

The fact is that the old-time Sussex man ate what he could get and his wife cooked it as best she could over a few sticks. She had no facilities and probably no energy for making pasties or plum cakes, for puddings or clotted cream, for scones or buns or tea bread. The first and most important thing was to fill one's stomach, which is not the best way to start a tradition of good cookery.

For Sussex has always been a poor county. Even in its industrial days, when the crimson banners of its furnaces and forges "streamed out into the blackness of the Tudor night," the wealth was all clutched into the fists of the furnace-owning families—the toiler at the bellows or at the cinder hill or at the sluice gates of the hammer ponds or in the fuel-bearing forests probably earned no more than the toiler in the fields and fed as poorly. When the furnaces had consumed all the vast forests that fed them, one by one they guttered down, turning the mine owners into impoverished landowners, the miners into field hands whom the red iron still mocked in the surfaces of untractable clay.

The county endured to the full the agricultural miseries of the eighteenth and nineteenth centuries, without the reliefs afforded elsewhere by the neighborhood of big manufacturing towns. It was not till Brighthelmstone had become Brighton and the fishing villages of Bourne and Bexhill had bloomed with their ancient castled neighbor into seaside resorts that Sussex was put on its legs by a new industry—an industry much more ruinous to the beauty and integrity of its countryside than all the slag heaps and cider hills of the furnaces.

But the Sussex character had already long been formed—in the old days of fields and forges, clay and iron. Indeed it might be said to be molded of those very things, and like them it does not change. Such changes as time brings are all on the surface, and deep below the surface lie those resistances which will never allow the Sussex man or woman to relax into the ways of other counties.

The fatalism engendered by centuries of struggle and (I fear) acceptance of defeat, still directs their lives. And it overflows the kitchen. There the Sussex cook is still in her own mind struggling with the inscrutable thwartings of nature. Suggest to her that she should control the heat of her oven and she looks at you as if you had asked her to control the heat of the sun. If anything goes wrong it is as if the weather had "turned off" and nobody is more to blame for the one than for the other. "It's the fish—it went like that," she explains when I lament an uneatable lukewarm mess; in similar words will her husband explain "It's the drythe" when his cauliflowers fail.

I try in vain to persuade her that obstacles can be overcome and failures avoided. Such ideas savor to her of an impious disregard of natural laws, and also, I think, of an ambitious style of cookery which it is unreasonable to expect of a cottage housewife. She cooks as she has always cooked, and believes as she has always believed that " these things can't be helped"—just as the gardener believes that we are condemned to lose two-thirds of our tomatoes every year from blight.

I sometimes wonder if the gates and railings, the andirons and fire irons, the cannon, demi-cannon, culverins and falconets that long ago were thumped into shape in the Sussex forges were always, or indeed often, successful in use. Certainly the specimens that have survived are very beautiful and have lasted long, but I imagine that here we have one more case of the survival of the fittest; and that besides these enduring types many others, more ephemeral, at one time existed, and have long ago crumbled back into their element.

Certainly it is a characteristic of the present-day Sussex man not properly to finish what he makes, or to leave out some important part of it. "I didn't trouble" is the sort of explanation—not apology—that one sometimes receives, to account for the fact that the last few yards of the hedge have not been "laid along" or the most virulent and proximate wasps' nest left untaken. Another characteristic which has sometimes amazed me is the complete indifference with which a craftsman will watch his work deteriorate or even fall to pieces for want of proper maintenance. A gate or a fence in which the maker has been really interested, and of which he has seemed proud, and for which he has been praised, is no sooner put up than it is allowed to fall down. Only the most constant goading will keep it in repair.

This being so, I think it probable that a great many early fire irons, gates and pales were burned out by insufficient processes and came to untimely ends. As for Master Huggett's famous cannon, I will wager that it killed more of those who fired it than of those it was fired at.

Master Huggett and his man John,
They did make the first can*non*.

The jingle conjures up a typically Sussex picture of a small private furnace, where the owner puddles about all day long, helped by his faithful yet critical man. They have no particular hours or plans, but they have an idea of making some sort of a petard. Master Huggett who can read—a little—directs the technical side of things, which John criticizes out of the superior knowledge which every Sussex workingman possesses over his employer.

They make a great many models, some of which burst on firing and some of which fall to pieces before they are fired. John takes the characteristic Sussex stance—immobile save for the hand that scratches the head. Master Huggett retires into the privacy of his forge and does likewise. When he comes out they are both agreed that the thing does not work too well at present, but are divided as to the improvements required. John says it wants more iron in its construction, and Master Huggett says it wants more withy. For weeks they argue and scrap and tinker, but in the end is born of their differences a monster—a ridiculous, pot-bellied monster of iron and basketwork, which can, however, lob without bursting an iron ball for nearly thirty yards. It is the First Cannon.

It is the ancestor of every field gun barking across the Rhine, of every 88mm reply—of every Howitzer roaring in its tent of rags and leaves—of every Bofors tower spitting against the tip-and-run murderers on the promenade—of every giant ack-ack rocket firer—of every monster-born monster in a charge of tanks—of every red-hot bellowing mouth that hurls death screaming across the miles . . . as the oak is in the acorn so were all these in that ludicrous First Cannon and in the Sussex heads that created it.

It is a terrible thought for our county—a terrible achievement for Master Huggett and his man John, I wonder if they knew—or know. . . . Doubtless before the Judgment Seat they will plead ignorance as their excuse. But I am not quite sure . . . Probably the First Cannon burst long before it reached the wars, and was, as I have said much more dangerous to those who fired it than those who were within range of the ball it vomited out of its iron-cum-osier belly. But I have very little doubt but that they made it as deadly as they could, and what can Howitzer or Gatling or Bofors do more?

I see them doomed by the Universal Justice to wander miserably through the fourth dimension, pushing a barrow and crying wearily "Any old iron?—any old iron?"—till they have collected the last bolt, the last splinter, the last rusty piece of scrap left by the last cannon fired on earth. Then perhaps hell will open and swallow up their huge, ghastly slag heap, and they will be allowed to set up in the New Jerusalem as honest blacksmiths.

5.

OUR SUBJECT IS CLOSER THAN IT SEEMS, FOR MY KITCHEN has often been darkened by the shadow of Master Huggett and his man John. Indeed, there have been times when the First Cannon has almost seemed a part of my kitchen battery. But those noisy episodes belong to my third year as cook, not to my first, which was quiet enough, except for a rare sneak-raider. I was able to plan and concentrate and work undistracted, and it was not long before my repertory of dishes had very greatly enlarged itself.

My ambition had been to enlarge rather than to exploit my knowledge. Even if it had been less limited I should still have wanted to expand, for variety is to me salt rather than spice. One of the main drawbacks of a professional cook is, as a rule, her lack of variety. She has a tendency to avoid dishes that have ever been failures or that give her much trouble and to concentrate on those which she knows she can make easily and well. It is true that I once had a cook who could work only from new ideas and grew tired of a dish when she had cooked it more than half a dozen times. But my experience is more normally represented by the cook who always triumphantly capped her unfailing suggestion of Shepherd's pie with "It makes a change, doesn't it?"

Being free of all this was one of the advantages of my lot. It is true that I had fallen into cookery just at the very worst period where raw materials were concerned— when rationing was tight, when utensils were scarce and when fuel could not be obtained without a permit or used without a guilty conscience. But at least I was free to make what I liked of these sad circumstances; I had not to endure another woman's defeatist campaigning. (I can hear the ring of joy in Norah's voice when in answer to my morning inquiry: "Well, what is there in the larder today?" she crooned, "Nothing at all, madam, nothing at all." I soon learned that "nothing at all" made a very good curry.)

My first act was to examine my cookery books, of which I had a number, and decide which would be of most practical use. I chose half a dozen. The first was a primer of cookery, the name of which I shall not give, as I have very little for it but abuse. The second was the time-honored and world-famous *Mrs. Beeton's Book of Household Management*. The third was *French Cooking for English Homes*, which I supplemented with Mr. Ambrose Heath's invaluable *Vegetables for Victory*. The fifth was a little brochure issued by the Frigidaire Company and called "The Silent Hostess." The last was incongruously but, as it happened, most usefully *Romary's Party Book* by Monsieur Boulestin. Though the consideration had not influenced me, I found that my choice had given me the advantage of three different conceptions and styles of cookery—the English, the French and the American.

The primer, as might be expected, was English. I had hoped it would give me the rudiments of cookery and genuinely enlighten my ignorance of processes and technical terms. What did one do, for instance, to "blanch" sweetbreads? How did one "fold in" the white of an egg? And how long did one cook sprouts?—five minutes?—twenty minutes?—an hour? The anonymous author did not tell me. He or she started off with an Arabian Nights' dream of what my kitchen stores should consist of, passed on to instructions as to the management of a gas cooker which I had not got, and then abruptly decided that I knew everything. He deigned to elucidate no terms—for these I had to go to the dictionary, which I found more helpful than I had expected—and the period of cookery was always "till tender," which to my ignorance might have been any period from three minutes to three hours.

The first result of my efforts to master the primer was a decision (afterwards modified into the present work) to write a cookery book of my own—a Mug's Cookery Book, which would lighten the darkness of females like myself driven by the fortune of war into the kitchen. Not for us lighthearted chat about blanching and folding or instructions to cook till tender. Tell us exactly what to do and how to do it, with a diagram if necessary; tell us the earliest time we should hopefully prod and the latest when we must give up hope and decide mournfully that someone has blundered.

Another result was more directly fruitful. The primer led me to consult Mrs. Beeton. For among the innumerable virtues of this lady is the fact that she always tells you how long everything should take to cook. "Time— 45 minutes" . . . "Time 2½ hours" . . . such instructions are invaluable to the beginner who apart from technical considerations, likes to know exactly at what time she should give up her gardening or her darning or her writing, and start preparing dinner. One is always going from one job to another, and hanging on to each till the last moment, so it is frustrating to find one has allowed an hour and a half to prepare what takes only forty mintues, or—my more common situation—to find oneself starting a two-hour job with only half an hour to go.

Mrs. Beeton has been widely abused as extravagant—she is supposed never to make a cake with fewer than half a dozen eggs. Actually I have caught her using an egg less than my primer. Of course my edition has been modified, and brought up to date; it has been stripped of much of its Victorian lushness and though its quantities undoubtedly are those of peacetime, one of the first things a wartime cook must learn is how to adapt peacetime recipes. I dislike wartime recipes—they always seem to me either defeatist, making the worst of a bad job with starchy messes, or else unwarrantably optimistic as to the results, say, of substituting vinegar for brandy in mince pies.

On the whole I have found Mrs. Beeton easier to adapt than other prewar instructors. She tells you so much about everything that even a beginner is able to grasp the essential theory of a dish and know what to leave out without detriment to the main idea. One does not, of course, after consulting her, profess to have produced *boeuf-à-la-mode* out of the remains of last Sunday's joint, but one has at least produced a more appetizing finale than if one had followed a wartime recipe for hash.

She provides, moreover, such a gorgeous variety of dishes that one has a wide choice even in wartime. In times of abundance there is no limit. Should you, for instance, wish to cook a kangaroo, there it is, to be jugged, curried or fricasseed according to your whim —with a swan, a bandicoot, or a wallaby for special occasions.

Another of her virtues is that nothing is beneath her notice—she will tell you how to make toast with the same care and good-will as she will tell you how to make an *omelette surprise*. She even deigns to explain her own terms; if I had gone to her first, instead of the primer, I should not have had to use a dictionary.

Her main extravagance is extravagance in labor. Even my 1923 edition presupposes a vast kitchen, with a roaring coal range, and an adjoining scullery where subsidiary menials do the jobs that you and I have to do for ourselves as well as the cooking.

"The Cook," says Mrs. Beeton, "is queen of the kitchen. The duty of others is to render her ready and willing assistance . . . the cook takes charge of the soups, fish and poultry; the kitchen-maid of the vegetables, sauces and gravies. The scullery maid waits on and assists the cook." Later on, as a concession to modernity, we are told that "in small households the cook sometimes engages to do the whole work of the kitchen."

I find my Mrs. Beeton fascinating literature—too fascinating, for when I lift down her weighty mass—weightier than the telephone directory, weightier than *Ulysses*—to look for a recipe, I am lost in a maze of attractive bypaths, and it may be half an hour before I am at my destination. Even the index is full of counterattractions. You want to know, perhaps, how to deal with a peculiarly tough-looking specimen of ox liver, which the butcher has sent in response to your cry for offal. But before you finally decide to give it to the cat you have been entertained by much enthralling information, not only about ox liver, but about every sort of liver including your own (cirrhosis of, passive congestion of, fatty degeneration of, waxy degeneration of). Lobster leads straight to Lockjaw—then Locks—and Lodgers, Melted Butter to Meningitis, Condiments to Confinements, Drop Cakes to Dropsy and Drowning, Elderberry Wine to Electricity and Emetics, Haddock to Hair-Wash. Ices to Infants (carrying, feeding, washing and wet-nurse). The movement ends only with the alphabet.

Who could resist following up the reference to "Groper, Head and Shoulders boiled"? I could not, though having done so, I remained unenlightened. For though I knew how to cook a groper's head and shoulders, I was no nearer having any idea of what a groper was, though some clue to its appearance had been given by the instruction that "great care should be taken of the immense gelatinous lips." This suggests that, whether it be flesh, fish or fowl, the groper is not beautiful; on the other hand, the cook is urged not to "spoil the shape of the head by boiling it too quickly" . . .

I came nearest to enlightenment when shutting up the henhouses one evening soon afterwards. It was dusk, almost dark, and as I walked up the field a pale mysterious shape floated against the background of the woods. It seemed to be a head and shoulders only . . . I gazed, peered closely. . . . Could this be? . . . Was I contemplating at last a groper? The idea was favored by the profile which displayed what appeared to be "immense, gelatinous lips." It had a round head and humped shoulders, and it moved in typical specter fashion, with a slow, gliding fall through the twilight—till suddenly it came to rest on a gatepost. Then my ghost story ended familiarly with the hoot of an owl.

So there is still an unanswered riddle in my life. Hang it all—what *is* a groper?

Mrs. Beeton, of course, has written no mere cookery book, but a Book of Household Management, and it is to that fact that its superior enchantment is due. She deals not only with the kitchen, but with every other room in the house, not only with the servants but with the mistress and not with her only but with her husband, her children, her afternoon callers, her doctor, her lawyer, her laundry . . . in fact simply everyone and everything that goes into the house either by the front door or the back.

I have said that my edition has been brought up to date, but I must thankfully add that this has not been done consistently. Afternoon callers still occasionally appear as "morning visitors" and the good old English word "dress" still functions in recipes. Of turnips, for instance, we are told that "unless nice and young, they are scarcely worth dressing"—a remark which the cynical might apply to others besides turnips.

Also, listen to my Mrs. Beeton on baths.

For purposes of cleanliness, the baths *par excellence* are those of warm water, this term being applied to those in which water of a temperature from 70° to 80° Fahrenheit is employed. Soap or alkali in some form is necessary to remove the fatty matter poured out by the oil glands . . . The frequency with which a warm bath should be repeated varies with different individuals. A safe rule is to bathe the body twice a week in winter and every other day in summer . . . the best time for a warm bath for those who are in robust health is in the evening. Invalids however and those of a delicate constitution will often find that they endure the exertion of taking a bath best about 11 o'clock in the morning, after the digestion of the morning meal is accomplished and before they are tired out with the fatigues of the day.

The illustrations, unfortunately, have been modernized. There are still, I am thankful to say, those marvelous plates of unbelievable dishes, which are as worthy of being framed and hung on the wall as many a fashion or flower plate of the same period. But the rooms, furniture, table decorations, etc., have all been brought forward into the late fumed-oak period and are uniformly depressing.

Mrs. Beeton gives recipes in the styles of all countries, but she remains typically and supremely the exponent of English cookery. This has been defined as a style which depends for its success on the excellence of the ingredients. It might also be described as the style which best sets forth that excellence. For instance, I cannot believe that there is a better way of cooking a really good joint of English meat, be it beef, mutton, pork or veal, than the English way of roasting it—for choice and unlikely chance on the spit, but failing that in the oven. Any other way of cooking it, be it never so skillful, I find disappointing. One has been given something clever instead of something good.

The same applies to really young, fresh vegetables, to trout and salmon straight from the stream, to spring chicken, partridges and grouse, to cakes and scones and pastry made of fresh dairy produce. There is nothing better. But we are faced with the dark side of all this—with the fact that if second-rate material has to be used the meal at once becomes not second-rate but fifth-rate; depending absolutely as it does on first-rate ingredients, nothing synthetic and nothing in the way of substitute will do.

I know that the market is, or was, full of synthetics and substitutes, but these are the things which have earned English cooking its bad name. They make for all the inferior cookery of hotels and restaurants which used to be such an amazement to foreigners—they and sheer ignorance and inexpertness on the part of the cooks, they and sheer lack of taste and interest on the part of the public. Broadly speaking, we are a nation without a palate; as in certain animals, the main process of a meal goes on only in our stomachs and not in our mouths. The average British workingman asks to be filled at all costs and the average British gentlewoman shamelessly boasts that she does not notice what she eats . . . so what can you expect?

Some of the results, no doubt, are useful in wartime. The Ministry of Food for instance, can tell the public that it will not notice the difference between an omelet made of dried eggs and an omelet made of fresh eggs and be speaking nothing but the sorry truth. But the main, permanent result can be described only as a criminal style of cookery, wherein the young, the lovely and the innocent are murdered—fried to cinder, boiled to a slop, smothered with burning sauces out of proprietory bottles, robbed of their flavor, their succulence, and their nutrition by the executioner in the kitchen.

Therefore to cling to English cookery during a war under the impression that because it is simpler it is easier under war conditions is a mistake of which the green cook should be warned, if her experiences have not already done so. Of course there is one ingredient of English cookery which remains as plentiful as ever and that is water. But water has at least this in common with fire, that, though a good servant it is a bad master, and *Cuisine Anglaise à l'eau* is a formidable addition to the horrors of war.

Moreover, English cookery is singularly unimaginative in dealing with "leftovers" which form so large a part of a wartime larder. I know that we have hash, and shepherd's pie, and even curry may perhaps be called an English dish; but leftovers cannot be regarded as first-class material and therefore are not really within the scope of real honest English cookery.

The Co-Optimists used to sing a song which went something like this—

> It's the roast beef of Old England
> Makes us do the things we do.
> Hot on Sunday, cold on Monday,
> Tuesday and Wednesday too
> We make it into Irish Stew.

I think we ought to forget all of this except the first two lines.

6.

LET US THEN BE ENGLISH ON SUNDAY, BUT FRENCH ON Monday—Tuesday and Wednesday too. French cooking has the reputation for making the best of a bad job. (Does there not exist the legend of a French cook who for a wager served up most deliciously the sole of an old boot?) Among the ignorant and insular it also has the reputation of disguising good food in unrecognizable messes; they speak contemptuously of "kickshaws," the word our ancestors made of the *quelque chose* which figured as a sweet dish on the tables of Elizabethan gourmets, when English cooking was more continental in style than it is now.

I have already said that for the fundamental excellence of meat and vegetables nothing is better than the plain English treatment of fire and (not too much) water. But one can weary even of excellence if it is too often repeated, and a monotonous diet is nearly as unwholesome for many people as an inadequate one. Besides, as I have said, the first-class ingredients are lacking. We are forced to fall back on the inferior and third-rate, on strange, uncomely parts of the animal whose legs and loins have exclusively fed us till now, on sinister offals, on withered and wilting vegetables, on fish the names of which we had not heard before the war.

French cookery will help us tackle all these, because it is truly democratic and never was in operation for only those who can afford the best cuts or Scotch salmon at six shillings a pound. I refer of course to the *cuisine bourgeoise*, not to the *haute cuisine* of exclusive hotels and the châteaux of industrialists. It is the style which is—or perhaps, alas, I should say, was—within the reach of every *petit bourgeois*. It presupposes, of course, a democracy which has never existed in this country, where before the war working-class housewives could not afford to buy fresh milk for their families—a democracy of butter, milk and wine.

So—you quite rightly exclaim—what on earth is the use of it now? At the time of writing, butter and milk are rationed, while as for wine, it is a dream—or indeed, more likely, should you succeed in getting hold of a bottle, a nightmare. The French, in substituting dairy produce for water as the chief medium of their art have made its practice impossible in times of scarcity.

This is true up to a point. If we are going to attempt even an emergency version of French cooking we must divert our dairy rations from the tea table. We shall have to cut down on cake making, to do with less milk in coffee and even in tea, to forego the convenience of a bread and cheese lunch, and spread our carpet of jam without the luxurious underfelt of butter or margarine. It is a question of choice—which would we rather have? A French dinner or an English tea? I personally have chosen the dinner, but I know a great many who would prefer the tea.

Yet even these need not entirely give up the idea of French cookery. Without using fats there are some variations on the eternal theme of water. Take rice, for instance. English rice is inevitably boiled in water, but a world of improvement can be made by boiling it in stock. I know that there are objections to this. I once asked an experienced cook to boil some rice in stock, and she replied that it was impossible.

"Why?" I asked.

"Because, after it is boiled I must pour lukewarm water over it to separate the grains, and that would also wash away the stock and all the flavor."

When I took over my own cooking I decided to boil my rice in stock even at the risk of some small detriment to its appearance. That is to say I boiled it, but did not afterwards pour lukewarm water over it to separate the grains. The difference in flavor was enormous, the difference in appearance scarcely noticeable. It is true that it did not look so white, having taken the color of the stock, but every grain was separate, just as if it had been watered.

Of course if you boil rice to a mush you may be able to retrieve it by washing it under the tap, but experience has taught me, a very green cook, that it is not difficult to boil rice so exactly right that it needs no further treatment. The point to remember is that rice seems to have two crises in its career—the first almost immediately after it is put into the saucepan, the second some fifteen minutes later, when it is nearly ready. If you stir it safely through these it will reward you by complete independence on the part of each grain. But even if it did not, I should still think an immaculate appearance a poor reward for the loss of flavor that boiling in water entails—only a degree better than the results of boiling soda with Brussels sprouts.

The point is that while English cooking is a profession, French cooking is an art. It is meant for those who will take trouble and make sacrifices for a result that goes very much deeper than appearances. The French housewife, even if she keeps a good cook, never puts herself into her hands entirely. She has her own ideas, her own inspirations; she knows, moreover, how everything is done and what the results should be. In the kitchen mistress and maid are equals, fellow artists, discussing freely all the ways and means of eating from the actual purchase of the food to its final consumption. No Frenchwoman would have given me the reply I received from an English hostess when I asked her how she had achieved such an excellent mayonnaise in wartime—"I really don't know. I leave all my stores to my cook."

A professional cook aims chiefly at pleasing her employer, who may be totally ignorant and quite unappreciative of her efforts, but is generally susceptible to appearances. How often when supplying a "reference" I have had to answer a question that I never ask myself —"Does she serve dishes attractively?"—or even, I fear, "daintily." I imagine that the average English employer would be entirely satisfied with a cook who sent to table tasteless but well-boiled rice and yet would find fault if the rice were dingy-looking or inclined to be sticky, though well-flavored. Indeed the English housewife has already decided that she would rather have rice deprived of nearly all its food value by polishing and blanching than eat it as it is eaten by millions of Eastern peasants who have no other diet, and would be dead in a month if they had to live on rice as it is sold in this country.

Contrary to popular opinion, French cooking is not for those who prefer looks to virtue. It often looks greasy and the "disguises" it is supposed to indulge in are disguises of flavor and substance rather than of appearances. Its main advantage in times of scarcity is, as I have said, its power to adapt itself to poor conditions and materials. It does this not only by its skill in flavoring but by its superior powers of nutrition. When you boil anything in water you have taken from, not added to its value as food; so to use water to cook inferior substances (such as English rice) or substances that have already been cooked, such as remains of meat and fish, is to reduce enormously the practical efficiency of your meal. Stock—by which I do not necessarily mean rich bone or meat stock, but stock made of meat or vegetable essence or even vegetable water—margarine, cooking fat, bacon fat, milk (we surely all of us can spare a little of these from time to time) will give our meals an increased sustaining power, as distinct from mere filling. French food is essentially blood-making; when overrich it can promote acidity, but there is not much fear of that under present conditions.

Its actual adaptation to a war situation is an easier matter than the adaptation of plain English cookery. Where there are only a few ingredients it is difficult to omit even one of them without spoiling the whole and a substitute immediately becomes noticeable. I acknowledge that the French dish is not always what it ought to be and certain gourmets might contend that to eat, say, chicken *à la marengo* without olive oil and mushrooms (or even indeed without chicken, if rabbit only is available) is worse than not to eat it at all. But I maintain that such an impoverished and improvised dish is better worth eating than the average wartime effort. We do not aim at producing a menu for gourmets but at feeding families who are sick of the limited resources of "plain" cooking, and have tastes that exclude as flavoring the merely "tasty."

Let me give as an example a risotto which is exceedingly popular in my own family, and superior both in flavor and as food to its English counterpart, and yet is sheer adaptation from start to finish. Perhaps I should not call it a French dish, for it is Italian in origin, a family recipe of the *diva* Grisi, who married Theophile Gautier. But I found it in *French Cooking for English Homes* with whose permission I quote it now.

Chop up finely two onions and cook them in a large piece of butter in an earthen pan or aluminum saucepan. Upon no account let them brown. Carefully sort out half a pound of Patna rice, removing all small grit or stones. It must not be cooked nor washed but must be thrown into the saucepan quite dry over a very quick fire. Turn the rice round and round in the saucepan with a wooden spoon, so that every grain of rice is covered with fat. Then pour over it a large breakfast cupful of good stock or gravy. Stir well and tnen add a small wineglass full of sherry or Madeira wine, sprinkle it over with two large spoonfuls of grated Parmesan cheese. Keep stirring from time to time, adding gradually by small instalments at least two pints of stock and nearly half a pound of cheese. Made with Gruyère instead of Parmesan, it is also good. Or make a compromise by using half of each cheese. It must be cooked at least three quarters of an hour, the grains of rice must be as separate as possible and not in the least pasty or sticky.

That is the dish as it exists in the World of Ideas. This is how it comes to earth in my kitchen.

First of all I cook the onion, not in "a large piece of butter" but in a small piece of margarine. There should be just enough to cover each grain of rice when it is turned round in the saucepan, and I have found that no more than an ounce suffices for this. The rice of course is only what one gets on one's points at the grocer's and knows no more of Patna than the cheese knows of Gruyère or Parmese. But the great point is that it is dry, and innocent of water as a medium either of cleansing or cooking. Throw it in, turn it over with your wooden spoon and then add your stock, which can be made of any good meat or vegetable essence.

Next in the recipe comes the wine and the overwhelming majority of us will have to leave that out, though it is a serious omission. Personally I treasure (though not too long or the dish will taste of methylated spirit) every dreg of wine that is drunk in the house—Algerian or *vin ordinaire* from a wine society we have belonged to for many years and which still is able to ration us with a very few bottles each year. It is certainly not as good as sherry or Madeira, but I find it very much better than nothing. This also applies to its use in soup.

So if you have a tablespoonful of Algerian wine or "Government Sherry" left over from a party, add it to the rice; but if you have not got it, never mind, for you will still have a very pleasant dish. The next thing is to sprinkle in your mousetrap cheese. These inferior materials will probably make your *risotto* a little more sticky than it would have been had you used those in the original recipe, but all the same you will find it much better flavored and more nourishing than any plain English "savoury rice." It is not, by the way, a dish which at any stage can be left to "cook itself." It needs a lot of care and attention and constant stirring, or the rice will burn, so do not undertake it unless you are prepared to give your mind to it. It is a piece of music you are playing yourself, all through, not a record on the gramophone, which you have only to put on and then switch off when it is over.

This characteristic sense of cooking as an art shows itself not only in inspiration but in the care, thought and attention devoted to each dish. It is also sometimes expressed by a curiously un-French indifference to what would appear to an Englishman important considerations of business and finance.

I remember lunching in a little restaurant at Chenonceaux. It was very small—only a few tables; Monsieur cooked and Madame did the waiting, but it had much more than a local reputation as a place *où on mange bien*. We had finished our lunch and the place was closing down when two cars pulled up at the door, and a young man sprang out, followed by a number of eager friends.

"*Madame,*" he exclaimed, "*voilà dix affamés qui vous supplient de les laisser manger ici.*"

But Madame shook her head. No, it was too late—the lunch was over. She had nothing to offer. They must go elsewhere. They pleaded, but in vain, and finally the two carloads departed to a more accommodating establishment.

My husband looked almost shocked.

"But couldn't she have made up something for them, even if her lunch was finished?—an omelet?—something cold? It's very bad business to turn away customers like that."

Our Breton car driver answered gravely.

"*Non, monsieur. Elle a à considerer la renomée de sa maison.* It would never do if afterwards one of these types was to say that he had eaten *chez elle* something improvised, something below her standard of cooking. She has the reputation for giving nothing but the best."

Could poetry or painting ask more of those who love them?

7.

THE TURN FROM FRENCH TO AMERICAN COOKERY IS as big a sweep round as the turn from English to French. To cook in three styles certainly makes for variety even under restrictions, and I have found American recipes as useful in wartime as French. The main reason for this is that, though sometimes exotic as to materials—many of the ingredients would be difficult to procure over here even in normal circumstances— American cookery is economical as to time and fuel.

Unlike English cookery, which fundamentally contemplates a whole-time salaried cook working at a kitchen range, or French cookery which demands a housewife who is willing to spend any amount of time, thought and energy in her kitchen with its stove that never goes out, American cookery envisages a housewife whose cooking is done in her spare time on a gas or electric cooker. Not for her those dishes that take hours to cook or cannot be left to "cook themselves." She will probably, too, want to fit the cooking for two or three days into a single morning, so that the rest of those days may be free for her job or her cultural and social engagements. The French cook would shrug her shoulders and look skeptical of such methods, the English cook would toss her head and look superior, but the fact remains that this is the method that was urged on English cooks throughout the war as one of the very best ways of saving time and fuel.

Of course the American housewife has her refrigerator, which is still a luxury in England and even more rare in France. But I must state frankly that though the refrigerator with its cold storage for perishable foodstuffs is essentially the housewife's friend and ought not to be a luxury in any home, it can—by abuse—become the housewife's enemy and is already in my opinion the bane of American cooking.

From New York to New Orleans I have eaten delicacies that have been frozen into almost complete tastelessness—strawberries, chicken, asparagus, soft-shelled crabs, all tasting very much the same through too prolonged a sojourn "on the ice." This phrase "on the ice" follows one round the States; it has the same meaning as our "in the larder," which indeed is what the icebox has become in most American homes.

When, owing to severe illness, I had to cancel on Saturday morning an engagement for a "banquet" on the following Monday night, I was told reproachfully that "the chickens were already on the ice"—on the ice three days, with an outdoor temperature hovering around zero! I should have been more surprised had I not a short while earlier complained at a famous New York restaurant that my chicken was tough and tasteless through being too long on the ice, and heard the waiter reply—"It's only been on the ice a week—you sure wouldn't eat a chicken that hadn't been on the ice a week." When I told him that normally the chickens I ate had not been on the ice at all, I expect he thought I was a fool.

In Charleston we enjoyed the Negro cooking, because Negroes, like Sussex people and myself, are scared of electrical devices. But I found that American visitors to these places did not share our satisfaction. "I'm disappointed in this Negro cookery," a charming New Yorker said to me. "I don't think it's at all what it's cracked up to be. We did very much better at Miami, where all the food came down by ice train from New York. You ate it straight off the ice."

But it would be ungracious to dwell overlong on the abuses of an invention which has been such a personal comfort to me. I cannot imagine how I should have lived without it during these last years, with their rare deliveries of perishable goods, which but for its cold lodging would have perished indeed. Moreover, it has given not only to me but to my neighbors the treat of an occasional ice cream. I have proclaimed my willingness to make ice cream for anyone who will provide me with its main ingredient—a tin of evaporated milk—and could every summer have done a thriving business as a hoky-poky merchant.

Here once again I have laid a bogey of the professional cook. How seldom have I enjoyed ice cream under her auspices, how unwilling has she always seemed to make it, how many difficulties has she always hinted at, and then in the end how many glassy thorns have always lain embedded in the creamy rose. I was given to understand that even the most constant stirring could not prevent the cream freezing into layers and splinters. One cook avoided these by passing the mixture through a seltzer siphon, but this, besides being an awkward business, always gave the ice a salty, soda-ish taste which was not pleasant.

It was not till I had followed a recipe for ice cream in my American cookery book, that I realized how simple the whole matter really was. I made a chocolate ice cream by boiling two tablespoons of unsweetened cocoa and a tablespoon of sugar in a cup of milk, then when the result had cooled folding it into a basin of evaporated milk whipped to the thickness of cream. I froze the mixture without stirring, and there were no splinters of ice in it—not the smallest fragment of one. Strawberries and raspberries put through the sieve or mashed with a fork provided later some delicious variations on this theme without any more trouble or any more splinters.

The reason for this must be the stratagem of substituting evaporated milk for the lost luxury of cream. Cream contains water, which during the freezing period can easily become separated and freeze into thin layers or needles of ice. The milk, on the other hand, is waterless and freezes entire. At least I imagine this to be the explanation, for in none of the numberless ice creams I have made, all without stirring and all without aerating, have I ever found the smallest shard. The results taste almost undetectably like cream, and I do not imagine that I shall ever feel tempted to return to an extravagance which makes on the whole less difference than difficulty.

It was my little American cookery book which told me that whipping will make evaporated milk into at least a tolerable imitation of cream (for cooking purposes, not, alas, as an accompaniment to strawberries). Actually I had already discovered this for myself, but having been told by more than one experienced person that it was impossible, I felt glad to have my own experience confirmed as valid.

The book has also taught me a number of other trouble-saving things, for it is written mainly from the angle of the cook who has also to be the hostess. The processes of cooking and serving are reduced to a simplicity which might work out a bit "thin" in ordinary times but are often all that is possible now. For instance, tomato consommé takes only half an hour to make, and by being then brought to the boil again with a leaf of gelatine becomes a heretical version of *consommé en gelée*.

Of course in a way it is all bogus, and perhaps even shocking to the true connoisseur, but I have found the results very much more appetizing than those of the usual wartime recipe, and the processes by which they are achieved are a boon to the busy cook and hostess. Only my little American book could have enabled me to serve with so little trouble and so much success in the midst of all our scarcities a July supper of cold jellied soup, chicken mousse and chocolate ice cream.

Another great advantage of American cookery where English people are concerned is its respectful regard for appearances. In no other country have I seen meals more attractively served. It is a formidable jolt to be transported from an American hotel where your breakfast arrives on a trolley wheeled in by two white-uniformed waiters—a trolley bright with snowy linen, with shining cutlery and perfect china and laden with rolls of divers sorts and butter, honey and orange juice in nests of cracked ice, and perhaps even a rose beside your plate—it is a formidable jolt to change from this to a tray the size of a pram wheel but weighing at least a ton which a waiter deposits suddenly on your bed or poises dangerously on the edge of your night table—a tray bringing you no more than two tough-looking rolls, a few dissolving pieces of butter, and a battered coffee-pot.

An American salad is a thing of beauty, though I never found an American salad dressing which did not betray the deepest convictions of the country of its origin. I soon gave up asking for a French dressing, and Russian and Scandinavian too when I found they tasted the same. But the salad itself, unless again it had tarried too long in the icebox, was always a delicious affair—tempting, varied, imaginative, and often a substantial meal.

The busy American woman commonly lunches off a salad, which would be starvation diet to her English sister with ideas seldom roaming beyond lettuce and a little cress. Yet what could be more timesaving, more food-saving, and more fuel-saving than a meal which requires no cooking and which uses up any leftovers that can be eaten cold by embedding them attractively in crisp green vegetation? The British wartime housewife lunching alone, like the heroine of Lady Peck's charming and so true *Housebound*, on the pooled remains of yesterday's meals heated up in a pudding basin, might surely take notice with profit both to her health and her economy.

Part III

Stretto

1.

WE NOW COME TO THE PART OF THE BOOK WHICH was originally intended to be the whole—to the Mug's Cookery Book boiled down to a single chapter. It is an occasion similar to that on which a hostess says meaningly to a female guest— "Come out with me for a moment" and mysteriously departs, leaving the rest of the company to kick their heels and entertain one another as best they can till she returns at the end of an hour. In this case my readers have wider opportunities, for they may skip to the next chapter or close the book altogether.

Mrs. Mugg and I go off into the kitchen and shut the door. We do not want any indifferent male or superior female to sneer at our stumbling efforts and humiliating confidences.

I still remember with shame that day now several years ago when I invited a busy inspector from the local agricultural committee to stop for a cup of tea. My cook and parlormaid were both out (I always gave them the same afternoon off for companionship's sake, though they fought like cats) and Mrs. Boorman who usually "ran in" on these occasions to make tea for us was not due for another half hour. I rather fancied the idea of myself making tea for my visitor, and as I knew he was in a hurry, I felt that I must not keep him waiting till my "help" arrived.

But how long the electric kettle was taking to boil! At least ten minutes had passed and the water was still quite cold. I waited another five minutes and then decided that something must be wrong. I looked at the switch. It was "on," so that could not be at fault. But there was no time to search out causes—I must at all costs obtain effects. So I found an ordinary kettle and put it to boil on the electric cooker; but that too seemed to hang fire. Long before it was more than warm Mrs. Boorman had appeared (at her appointed time) and discovered what the reader has no doubt guessed, that though the main switch of the cooker was on I had not switched on the kettle. As for the electric stove I had never turned the plate above "low." It is to people like that that I address the following remarks.

My purpose is to give some recipes in language that even the most ignorant mug can understand. Possibly by the time this book appears there will be no mugs left, as time and experience will have eliminated the last. Yet in case some should still survive in sheltered spots where cooks have lingered until after the war, I offer a few suggestions that have helped me personally.

Does anyone ever use the recipes to be found in books and newspapers? A well-known publisher once told me that one of his editors had sought to enlarge the scope and circulation of a literary magazine by publishing a weekly cookery hint. No sooner had the first appeared than someone rang up the office to say that the combination of ingredients suggested was in fact poisonous and that anyone who ate the dish was likely to be taken ill, if not to die. There followed a considerable stir, for the magazine had already been some days on the bookstalls. Booksellers were rung up and urged to trace all the copies that had been sold—this was before the days of broadcasting—the police were warned and I am not sure that the town crier was not sent out in some places. Having done their best to avoid mass murder the publishers settled anxiously to await news of the first casualties. None came. It was confirmed that the recipe was undoubtedly poisonous, but as there were no complaints and no catastrophes, the obvious conclusion was that nobody had tried it. The publishers gave up the idea of cookery as an encouragement to literature.

I can guarantee that none of the following recipes is poisonous, because I have eaten the results of them all without any ill effects. But I seriously urge mugs to remember that certain combinations of certain separately harmless ingredients can be unwholesome, if not actually dangerous. I shall not easily forget the question I once heard a woman ask another—"Tell me, did your mincemeat look at all different from usual before it blew up?" Sometimes at the start an enthusiastic soul is apt to be too enterprising and call too generously on her imagination. To be proudly told, as I have been, that "this soup contains beer and treacle" is not reassuring to the dyspeptic guest, nor is he or she likely to welcome the announcement "It is all my own invention." The White Knight often has too free a hand in the amateur kitchen.

So Mrs. Mugg and I will be very sober cooks, though our recipes will not be of the soberest kind, for reasons I have given in the preceding chapter. Some women when they start to cook think they will be safer if they stick to very plain dishes—cottage pie, Irish stew, fried or boiled fish, boiled puddings. But though it is possible to produce something like these even in wartime, they are none of them foolproof nor, in fact, actually easy. A dish is not necessarily easy to cook because it is "plain"; and as I have already said, there is nothing like plain food for stressing substitutes and scarcities.

Here I must say a few words about my ingredients. I have no doubt certain advantages in this line—certain raw materials which many of my readers will be without. I keep rabbits and I keep hens; hence I have all the rabbit meat I want and usually a good supply of what I have now learned to call shell eggs. I also have a large and well-stocked kitchen garden.

I suspect that many readers will be inclined to envy me these so simple, so priceless, possessions, and as I cannot bear to be envied I will now pass on to the things I am without. I have no more bacon, butter, cream or cheese than other people, because unfortunately and improvidently we do not keep pigs or cows. I am registered only at my village shop, which though it gives me a warm personal interest in addition to willing service is not able to supply much in the way of extras. I am also short of cooking utensils. When my last cook departed and I took stock of what she had left behind, I found an alarming number of saucepans in holes or spoiled by neglect or burning. I could have forgiven her and her predecessors for this; what I could not forgive them was their not having told me, for some of the casualties looked of very early date and had I known about them at the time I could easily have found replacements. As things were I had to go out into the middle of a saucepan famine and tramp myself literally to lameness before I found a small cast-iron receptacle (holding at most a pint and weighing at least a hundredweight) and had my name put down for another at some uncertain date. On these and a few battered survivors I have to make shift.

But my crowning shortage is for most people a common abundance. I am short of water. I cannot blame the war for this, which is an odd sensation. Water has always been a difficulty and two years of drought emptied our main well in the autumn of 1943, leaving us with a subsidiary one which seems never either to run dry or to contain more than two feet of water. Some years ago we decided to clean it, because the district analyst had reported animal life therein and his report had been hideously confirmed by the draw-bucket. But when we tried to empty the well for this operation we found that the most strenuous efforts of four strong men were unable to pump it dry. The water streamed out of the pump lines for hours, but there were always those two feet at the bottom. So we gave up the idea and followed instead the example of Aunt Maria's nephews in the *Ruthless Rhymes*.

> In the drinking-well
> (Which the plumber built her)
> Aunt Eliza fell
> We must buy a filter.

We are, of course, in a common rural predicament, and many of our neighbors are worse off than we are. The countryside is used to being without water, and for the most part cottages are content to use only a few pailfuls a day and to carry these long distances —hanging from wooden shoulder-yokes like a Victorian milkman's—from whatsoever well or pond may still be "in production" during a drought. When we made our first outcry about lack of baths we were told that "people don't come into the country to have baths" and that our well had never run dry "in the old days," when there was only one tap in the house. It was our "sinks"—i.e. washing basins—in the bedrooms that had done the damage. Indeed our dislike of washing by installments out of small jugs was regarded as altogether a deplorable sign of decadence.

A private water company's scheme for extending its mains to our village had some years earlier produced a reaction that would have been creditable had the threat been one of enemy invasion. The village refused to surrender. The company renewed its attack shortly after our arrival, and by that time the place had been infiltrated by fifth columnists in the shape of innkeepers who wanted to let rooms and various "gentry" who had long grown weary of bathing in the waters of a certain duckpond (sent round in a wheeled tank and smelling even worse hot than when cold). To quote one of the older inhabitants, our village "gave in" and the water was made available to such as would have it—by no means everyone. A later effort to bring the supply across the fields to a hamlet still nearer to us—which would have meant the end of our troubles, since we could have piped the rest of the way ourselves—has so far failed to penetrate local defenses.

These famines and frustrations produce at times a state

of mind in which I need to have recourse to Mr. Bennet of *Pride and Prejudice*. You remember the conversation with Mrs. Bennet, in which she says: "If it were not for the entail, I should not mind it." He asks: "What should not you mind?" and she answers: "I should not mind anything at all." To which he replies: "Let us be thankful that you are preserved from a state of such insensibility."

I have found this duologue the greatest comfort in times of stress and an unfailing stimulant to my morale. Whenever I begin to whine—whether it has been at the blackout, the fishmonger, fly-bombs, quaint Algerian mutton, hens that prate but do not lay, or the fact that our kitchen tap water tastes of musty cheese—"If it wasn't for these things I shouldn't mind"—then Mr. Bennet is at hand with his "What should not you mind?" and the spell of self-pity is broken.

His cynicism is more than ever healthy when I whine because some common, customary thing is lacking. Let us indeed be thankful that I am preserved from a state of insensibility to poverty—in this case my own, but extending, I hope, to the poverty of others. Too many of us have never been poor, and as a result have not always been guiltless of advising those without bread to eat cake.

When I was a girl I was often short of pocket money and had to go without cake, but I was never poor in the sense of lacking bread. And ever since I made some sort of a success for myself as a writer I have been able to afford even all the cake I wanted—a merciful Providence having preserved me from wanting such creamy luxuries as yachts, diamonds, ermine, large estates or villas on the Côte d'Azure. I certainly did not have to go without such ordinary confectionary as new books, new clothes, new furniture, servants or holidays or anything I specially wanted to eat and drink or cook with.

Then war came and the cake disappeared, or else existed in such small quantities that life became a struggle both to acquire it and to make it go far enough. And soon not only cake but bread was in short supply. I had to live as if I were poor; not desperately poor, nowhere near the poverty in which many citizens of this country lived before the war, but respectably poor—not well off, not comfortable. I had to go short of meat and sugar and fats and household equipment—I had to use towels and dusters after they were in holes and long past mending; my clothes and my furniture became shabby; my house—after several "near misses" from bombs and doodle-bugs—began to crack and bulge and let in the weather as badly as a slum attic.

It is right that I should in this way share the experience of so many of my fellow countrymen, who a few years ago did not go short because consumer goods were in short supply (in fact they were a glut) but because they had not the money to buy them. How many of us felt for them then? I fear that most well-situated women swept them conveniently out of their thoughts, or else subscribed to the humbug of "passing rich on forty pounds a year." Three pounds a week was considered amply sufficient for a workingman's family by people who must have spent at least twice that sum on food alone; and women who during the war would be almost in tears when the milk ration reached its winter solstice, were content to accept or—more likely—to ignore the fact that many workingmen's wives could not afford even to give fresh milk to their children. Well, at last we know; and I hope we don't forget.

2.

BUT NOW TO CUT THE CACKLE . . . HERE ARE THE OSSES. We will draw up, Mrs. Mugg and I, a complete menu, starting with the soup. I find soup such a good friend in the kitchen that I cannot help being astonished by its general neglect. In many well-to-do homes it is served only occasionally, while in those homes which in other European countries would rely on it as a main dish, it is almost unknown.

Shortly after last Christmas a farm laborer's wife came to me with the carcass and bones of a chicken.

"These are for you," she said. "It's the bones of our Christmas chicken, and we know you like soup." (Her mother would have called it "shackles.")

"But," I cried, "I can't possibly take your chicken bones. It would be robbing you. You and your family can have a most delicious meal off this."

She shook her head.

"We don't like soup," she said, "not chicken soup. Some of them don't mind potato soup, but not those other kinds. If you don't take these bones they'll only go to the cat."

Needless to say I took the bones, but I made the soup with a guilty conscience—vicariously guilty since it was obviously not I who had rejected good food. But it seemed almost shameful that only the circumstance of my living near had prevented these bones being given to the cat.

I serve soup every day. It is filling, nourishing, and a most practical and appetizing way of using up the remains of earlier meals. Say that you have some cottage pie left over—not enough to serve again, even if that would not be too depressing. Mash it up and put it in a saucepan with a little stock—add perhaps an onion or a carrot or a bit of what you fancy. Simmer for half an hour and then push through a sieve. Add some curry powder now and a little milk and you will have a very pleasant soup that has given you scarcely any trouble and used up nothing precious.

Of course if you have an electric or gas cooker you must forget all you ever heard about soup simmering for hours. Believe me, the most delicious soup can be begun and finished in an hour or less. On the other hand, if your soup really must cook long and slowly, as in the case of my chicken bones, it is not difficult to arrange for it to share with some other dish any hot plate that may be in use. The slower it cooks the better. I started my chicken soup the day before I wanted it, moving my saucepan about the top of the stove to any cooking space where there was room; then I left it overnight, and started on it again the next day. I am not saying that the method is ideal, but in this case it certainly produced the most delicious soup with scarcely any extra consumption of fuel. By a similar contrivance you can cook soup in the oven.

I am assuming today that Mrs. Mugg wants to use only raw materials, and we decide to embark on a diminished variety of *potage bonne femme*. The first thing to do is to have all the ingredients and utensils ready. Tragedies may be precipitated by having to search for milk or peel an onion at the critical moment. So put the following articles on the kitchen table before you do anything else.

Utensils. 1. A saucepan big enough to hold a quart and yet be only half full. You want to make soup for four people, and half a pint is plenty for each and allows for reduction in cooking. If the saucepan is full there is some danger that you, being a mug, will let it boil over and make a mess, so it is wisest to fill it only half. 2. A grater. 3. A wooden spoon. Never use a metal spoon for soup, or indeed for most things. 4. A teacup.

Ingredients. 1. Two large potatoes. 2. Three medium-sized onions. 3. A small stick of celery (if obtainable, but the soup tastes very good without it). 4. A pint of water and a pint of milk. But if you cannot manage the latter, the proportions can be varied to a pint and a half of water and half a pint of milk. Or you can use Household Milk. Remember that a breakfast cup roughly measures half a pint and a teacup a quarter of a pint or a gill. 5. Small piece of margarine. 6. A tablespoonful of flour. 7. Pepper and salt.

Procedure. Grate up your potatoes and onions

on the large side of the grater. This is a good way out of the usual dainty dicing, which takes more time, more trouble, and more fuel. Melt your margarine in the saucepan. (A more experienced cook would do this while she was grating the vegetables, but you had better do one thing at a time.) When the margarine is making the sizzling noise which shows it is ready for cooking, put in the vegetables and put on the saucepan lid. Make sure that the heat is very low. (The prewar recipe requires a large piece of margarine, if not butter, and the tossing of the vegetables in this for twenty minutes, tossing and turning them continually with a wooden spoon to ensure that they do not brown. My expedient involves their cooking partly in their own steam and for not more than ten minutes, or they *will* brown. Shake the saucepan from time to time in case they stick to the bottom, and you may peep in occasionally, if you feel nervous, just to make sure that nothing untoward is happening.) Pour your water—hot or cold—over the vegetables, add seasoning and turn up the heat a little, but do not let them cook fast. Simmer—that is, let them cook with a slight movement of the fluid, not the bubble and bounce of boiling—until the vegetables are quite soft, which, as they are grated, will not take much longer than twenty minutes.

Now this would be the time to put the whole thing through a sieve, if you want to follow the normal English custom. But personally I prefer this kind of soup unsieved. Certain sorts you must sieve —pea soup, for instance, or soup made of leftovers —but I think this continental kind of soup tastes better if you eat it the continental way, that is with the vegetable shreds floating in it. If you sieve, do not add the seasoning till afterwards, as the flavor of it will probably remain on the wrong side of the sieve. On the other hand, if you are making a soup with, say, a flavoring of bacon rind, you must put

·[89]·

this in at the start and though it will not actually go through the sieve the flavor of it can be *pushed* through if you crush it well against the wires. Bacon rind is a great improver of the flavor of many soups, especially potato soup.

Having now decided whether to sieve or not to sieve, your next step is to thicken the soup with a little flour. Put this in a cup and add just enough milk to make a paste. Stir until it is quite smooth and then add a little more milk and stir again. Be sure there are no lumps, and do not pour it in all at once or over a hot fire, but add it gradually with the saucepan over a low heat. Then add the rest of the milk, turn up the heat and stir with a wooden spoon till the soup is thick and boiling. Do not on any account leave it to take care of itself at this stage—it needs watching and stirring, that is if you want a soup which is both smooth and thick.

This is as near as you can get in these days to a genuine *potage bonne femme*, but you can vary the recipe by adding bacon rind to the vegetables (at the start) or two tablespoons of grated cheese (at the finish—after it has ceased to boil). Or you can substitute leeks for the onions.

Now let us pass on to the next course, for which I have four suggestions.

1. A way of cooking fish (if you can get it).
2. A way of cooking rabbit (if you can get it).
3. Homemade noodles and tomato sauce.
4. The remains of your Sunday joint fried in *sauce piquante*.

The way of cooking *fish* is my own invention and involves for complete success some dregs of wine and a few mushrooms, either fresh or dried.

Utensils. 1. A baking dish. 2. Piece of greased paper large enough to cover it. 3. A saucepan for cooking the mushrooms. 4. A strainer. 5. A pudding basin. 6. A wooden spoon.

Ingredients. 1. Eight fillets of plaice (if again we are cooking for four people). 2. A dozen mushrooms. 3. A tablespoon of white wine. 4. A breakfast cup of milk or milk and water. 5. One large or two small onions, or (preferably) shallots. 6. A bay leaf. 7. The yolk of an egg or reconstituted egg powder. 8. Two ounces of margarine. 9. A tablespoon of flour. 10. A teacup of water. 11. Pepper and salt.

Procedure. First melt half your margarine in the saucepan over a low fire and put in the mushrooms, which of course you have skinned. If these are dried mushrooms you must soak them first in water for about three hours. (I dry mushrooms every summer by the simple process of putting them, after I have removed the skins and stalks, on a wire tray in my linen cupboard, as far from the hot pipe as possible, for they should dry very slowly.) Cover the saucepan and let them cook for ten minutes over a low heat, then add the water and let them simmer slowly till they are soft but not disintegrating, which will take about another ten minutes if they are young and fresh, but longer if they are old or have been dried. While they are cooking you can peel and chop up your onion.

You are now ready to start the main business. Grease your baking dish by rubbing it over with a tiny piece of fat or even with greasy paper in which fat has been wrapped. Then lay in your fillets. Try to persuade your fishmonger to remove the orange-spotted mackintosh which is part of a plaice's characteristic outfit and which he always seems to leave on the bottom fillets, possibly as a guarantee of their genuineness. If he has not done so, I do not advise you to try to remove it yourself, unless you are cleverer at these things than I am. I am told that by pouring boiling water drop by drop on the skin it is possible to take it off without pulling the fillet to pieces, but as the fishmonger has more experience, more dexterity and sharper knives than any of us I definitely think that it is his job.

Having laid the fillets on the dish, add the bay leaf and the chopped onion and then pour over them two tablespoons of the mushroom liquor, a tablespoon of wine, and a cup of milk. Add pepper and salt and cover completely with a piece of greased paper. Then put the dish in a moderate over and cook slowly for a quarter of an hour. I heat my oven to just under 400, and then switch off when I have shut in the fish.

While the cooking is in progress you may reconstitute and beat your egg. Then after fifteen minutes take the fish out of the oven and strain off the liquor into a pudding basin. Keep the fish hot while you make a sauce by melting the rest of your margarine in a saucepan and stirring in a tablespoon of flour. Add the fish liquor gradually, stirring all the while till in a few minutes the sauce is thick. Cook a minute or two longer and then take the saucepan off the fire before adding the beaten yolk of an egg. Whatever you do, do not add this over the fire or if the sauce is boiling, or the whole thing will curdle at once. Pour the sauce over the fish and arrange the mushrooms on the top before serving.

When he has eaten this dish your husband will probably tell you that he prefers grilled sole. So do you, so do I, so does almost anybody. But the point is that we are cooking plaice, which is one of those fish that are all the better for a little disguise. I should not dream of disguising the natural beauties of sole with mushrooms, onions and wine. Plaice is a very good fish, but not so good that we want to fry it every time we have it, and in my part of England we have it very often—in fact at the present moment it seems to be the only fish in the sea. Other kinds of fish can be cooked this way—cod, brill or skate—and if you have not, as is quite probable, any mushrooms or wine, you can still poach the fish in the milk, with the onions and bay leaf, or you could add some grated cheese to the sauce.

The next dish under consideration also provides obstacles in the way of ingredients, but this time it is the core and center of the whole thing that is in short supply. It has been a mystery to many people why rabbits which before the war were a plague throughout the countryside and so common and cheap in the shops as to be despised as food by the masses, should now, when they are most needed, have almost entirely disappeared —wiped out apparently with government approval.

The fact is, of course, that you cannot keep crops and rabbits on the same ground, and where wastelands and "bad old" fields have been turned into rather surprised-looking arable the rabbits have had to be got rid of by methods more drastic than trapping, shooting or even netting. They have also been systematically poached; as a result wild rabbits are almost unprocurable even by country dwellers. My rabbits are all tame and to anyone who lives in the country or has a fair-sized kitchen garden I cannot recommend a better, easier or cheaper way of stocking the larder. The meat of a tame rabbit is superior to that of a wild one, in quality as well as quantity. In the case of young ones it is not unlike chicken—I can still make a very passable chicken mousse. Indeed before the war my cook used always to make chicken mousse of rabbit, for the flavor of the genuine chicken is apt to be too slight and delicate for this purpose.

So, if you have rabbit, here is a very good way of cooking it. If not, something may be attempted on similar lines with liver, or with that mysterious and resistant substance known as "skirt."

Utensils. 1. A frying pan. 2. A fireproof casserole. 3. A wooden spoon or some other gadget for turning over the pieces of rabbit in the frying pan,

and a spatula for transferring them to the casserole.
4. A flour dredger.

Ingredients. 1. A rabbit, skinned and jointed. 2.
Two rashers of bacon. 3. Two fair-sized onions. 4.
Two fair-sized carrots. 5. About a pint of stock (if
you make it with meat essence, do not make it too
strong). 6. A bouquet of herbs, that is a sprig of
thyme, a sprig of parsley and a bay leaf. 7. Half a
dozen peppercorns. 8. A tablespoon of wine dregs
(if possible). 9. Seasoned flour in the dredger. 10. An
ounce of fat for frying.

Procedure. First dredge your pieces of rabbit
with seasoned flour, while you are melting the fat
in the frying pan. You can use any sort of fat, but
if you have only mutton fat, I should dilute it with
some of the rationed cooking fat or lard, as my
experience is that mutton fat will taste through anything. If you are lucky enough to have some beef
dripping it will greatly improve the flavor. When
the fat is giving out clouds of smoke, *not* before,
put in your pieces of rabbit and your two rashers of
bacon and fry them together for a few minutes, till
the bacon is cooked but not crisp, and the rabbit
lightly browned on both sides. Then take them out
and put them in the casserole while you fry your
onions, cut in quarters. Put these also in the casserole, with the carrots, cut in slices, and the bouquet
of herbs. Then pour in the stock and the wine if
you have any and put on the lid. Put the casserole
in a moderate oven (not more than 400) and cook
slowly till the liquid begins to move. Then reduce
the temperature of the oven still further by turning the heat right off and if necessary leaving the
door ajar for a few minutes. The point is that your
rabbit must cook very, very slowly. It will take about
an hour and a quarter or an hour and a half;
unless it is really old and tough, when you will have
to give it longer. Take out the bouquet of herbs

before serving. I always have mine tied to a piece of string.

My third dish has no obstacles in the way of ingredients. You can now buy noodles in the shops, but when I learned to make them you could not buy even macaroni or spaghetti, and anyway homemade noodles are much better to eat than bought ones.

Utensils. 1. A pastry board and rolling pin. 2. A mixing basin. 3. A wooden spoon for mixing. 4. A saucepan for making the tomato sauce. 5. A sieve and another pudding basin. 6. A cheese grater. 7. A sharp knife for cutting.

Ingredients—For the noodles: 1. A breakfast cup of flour. 2. A teacup of milk. 3. An egg, shell or reconstituted, but if real, use the yolk only. 4. Salt. For the sauce: 1. Six tomatoes, fresh, bottled or tinned. 2. Two onions. 3. A small piece of dripping for frying. 6. Half a pint of stock. 7. Pepper and salt and a teaspoonful of sugar. 8. You will also want about two ounces of grated cheese.

Procedure. Put your flour in the mixing basin with the dried egg powder, but if you are using a fresh egg yolk, add it with the milk. I suggest this to Mrs. Mugg rather than the more tricky process of starting with the flour on the pastry board, and then adding the egg and the milk by pouring them into a hole in the middle of the mass. Mix your ingredients in the basin with a knife rather than a spoon, as this is less sticky. Mixing and kneading dough is not without snags for the beginner, simple as it sounds. The first time I made noodles I soon found myself connected by ectoplasmic rods with half the surrounding furniture. When I struggled to the sink to turn on the taps, these too became involved, and altogether it was a shockingly sticky experience—due to my having made my dough too soft. It is best to add the milk gradually, till the dough is of the consistency of plasticine—firm and yet malleable. You must of course sprinkle the rolling board with flour, and I should put some on your hands and on the rolling pin too.

Roll out the dough very, very thin—the proper Italian recipe says "as thin as a mouse's ear." Then put the whole thing out to dry in the sun, or failing any sun, in the linen cupboard. It will take from one to two hours to dry and it must not be too dry, for it must be soft enough for you to be able to wrap it round your rolling pin without its breaking. Wrap it round and round and then pull out your roller. You must now cut the hollow roll into thin strips with a very sharp knife. Shake out the strips and you have your noodles. They will not perhaps look so elegant as shop noodles, but in flavor and freshness they will be far superior.

While the dough is drying you can make the tomato sauce.

Melt the dripping in a saucepan and then fry the onions in it till they are a golden brown. Cut your tomatoes into quarters and add them to the onion. Good tomato purée can be substituted for whole tomatoes if you like. Then pour in the stock, add the seasoning and let the whole thing simmer very slowly for an hour. Then push it with a wooden spoon through a fine sieve into a pudding basin. If the tomatoes are very juicy, as they sometimes are when bottled, do not add the full quantity of stock. But it is a great improvement to add a little rather than cook the tomatoes entirely in their own juice; so if the whole thing seems too liquid, pour some of the tomato juice away and keep it for soup.

When everything is ready cook your noodles by throwing them into a saucepan full of boiling, salted water. They will be ready in about ten minutes, for freshly made noodles take about a quarter of the time that shop noodles take to cook. But do not consider them ready till you have sampled one of them, to make sure that they are done enough.

Then put them in a hot fireproof dish and sprinkle the grated cheese all over them before you pour on the tomato sauce. If you have any leftover scraps of meat or sausage you may heat these up in the sauce before adding it, and your dish will be extra nourishing, though it is very good even without the meat.

Remains of meat have an important part to play in my next dish. In this you require—

Utensils.   1. A mixing bowl. 2. A frying pan. 3. A wooden spoon. 4. Three different-sized spoons for measuring.

Ingredients.   1. A tablespoon of salad oil. 2. A tablespoon of Lee and Perrins' sauce or something similar. 3. A dessertspoon of sugar. 4. A teaspoon, or less if you don't like things "hot," of mustard. 5. Half a teaspoon of salt. 6. Some leftover meat cut into small pieces.

Procedure.   First measure all your ingredients into a pudding basin. And here I should like to say a word about measuring. All the experienced cooks I know—and indeed many others—declare that they never measure, would get muddled if they did, and show a certain contempt for those who do. It is certainly unnecessary for any cook to measure foodstuffs with the same exactness as the grocer from whom she buys them, and there are so many qualifying circumstances as to the age, condition, consistency or state of preservation of any ingredient that it is as great a mistake to be slavishly bound to one's scales as to one's clock. But I submit that a beginner *must* measure until she really knows what quantities are. Some people learn this quicker than others; some never really learn it. I have known an experienced cook wreck a dish with false quantities. Do not worry about too much exactness, about quarters and eighths of an ounce, but use your spoons and your scales until you are quite sure of yourself and never mind what the superior cooks do or say.

When all your ingredients are in the basin, stir briskly with a wooden spoon. You have of course exclaimed that you have no salad oil, therefore the whole thing is impossible from the start. So it would be if there were no such thing as medicinal paraffin. I confess that this is my substitute, both in sauces and salad dressings; and up till now there have been no "incidents." It is not of course anywhere near as good as real olive oil, because it is absolutely flavorless, but it is just as efficient as far as cooking properties are concerned. Do not, of course, use it wildly. Your salad dressing will have to be made with a slightly lower proportion of oil than in the usual recipe. But your tablespoonful here will be undetected either by its flavor or its effects.

When you have mixed your sauce dip all the pieces of meat in it and fry them gently for fifteen minutes. This dish is greatly improved by adding an onion, and if so you must fry that first for a few minutes, chopped up, in a very little fat, before adding the meat.

We have now disposed of the main part of the mug menu, and there remains only the sweet. Most puddings have the same drawback as cakes in that they devour points and rations if one makes them properly, and the "austerity" substitutes are not, in my opinion, worth the trouble and the fuel.

Personally I am lucky in having—at least in summertime—a good supply of fresh fruit, and we eat this in the only way fresh fruit should be eaten, that is ripe and raw. An exception is made of the gooseberries, which are delicious stewed *when they are very young*—arsenic green in color and no more than a narrow eclipse between top and tail. Put them in a covered jar or pudding basin, with two tablespoons of sugar and a small cup of water, and stand them in a saucepan with boiling water reaching about two-thirds of the way up the jar. Simmer for twenty minutes, when your gooseberries should be tender. If they take much longer than this they are too old and should be left on the bush till they are ripe and can be eaten raw.

I also make fresh fruit salad, sometimes adding chopped dates to save sugar. Prepare your salad some time before you want it, sprinkle on the sugar and let it stand in a cool place to sweeten and make juice. A very agreeable salad can be made, too, of dried fruits—dates, prunes, sultanas, raisins, figs, apple rings, anything you are able to get hold of, with perhaps a spoonful of golden syrup or a spoonful of honey in the juice.

Baked apples can be improved by pushing a date into the empty core with a teaspoonful of sugar and a dab of margarine. Stewed plums, whether fresh or bottled, are much the better for the addition of mixed spices, which give them a rich, "pickled" flavor. But my favorite stewed fruit is the humble blackberry, for this—with the possible exception of the mulberry—is the only fruit I know which is improved in flavor by cooking. It also requires less sugar than most other fruit, and when bottled can in an emergency be eaten straight out of the bottle, without preliminary stewing.

If you want a change from fruit or cannot get any, something may be done with coffee essence or cocoa. I recommend coffee essence to the beginner, as it is much easier to manage than real coffee, though the flavor may not be so good. Dissolve a leaf of gelatine (or a heaped teaspoon of gelatine powder) and stir it into half a pint of milk which you have brought to the boil (stirring all the while) with two tablespoons of coffee essence and "sugar to taste." Then pour it into a mold and leave it to set. Or for the coffee substitute two tablespoons of sweetened cocoa, adding half a teaspoon of vanilla essence, if you fancy it—which I don't. It is all quite agreeable, if ordinary.

There is, however, one crisis to be feared. When first I made this mold, shape, or (if you are a restaurant) cream, it refused to come out of the jelly mold except as a horrid mess. The reason was that I had not rinsed the mold first with cold water, so that the mixture had stuck to the sides. I must confess, however, that I am exceedingly awkward at shaking creams or jellies out of molds. They steadfastly refuse to emerge, shake I ever so wildly, whereas for almost anybody else the same concoction will slide forth in immaculate contours. I do not know why this is, so I am afraid I cannot help you if you are in the same fix, except to advise you that your husband can probably do it. He could not make the thing to save his life, but that does not prevent him from being able to shake it. They are two unrelated accomplishments.

If gelatine is not too much of a problem, delicious jellies can be made of almost any fruit juice or fruit pulp. But if you want to add any of the whole fruit, remember to let the thing set a little before you put it in, otherwise it will all sink at once into a heap at the bottom. Of course if you are ever able to spare a teaspoon of rum, your range and effect are both enormously increased. You can concoct a rum cream in the same way as with chocolate or coffee; a drop of rum makes stewed fruit simply delicious, with the added advantage that you require very little indeed—for the flavor in this case should be unrecognizable except by an expert.

I suppose that Mrs. Mugg wants to make pastry, but let her be warned that not only is good pastry one of the most difficult performances for a beginner, but it is a devourer of fats, so that any failure is sheer catastrophe. Personally I would rather not eat pastry at all than follow an austerity recipe, with the single exception of one by Mr. Ambrose Heath, with which I economically vary Mrs. Beeton's "rich short crust." I have rations only for two, but perhaps Mrs. Mugg is more fortunate; so here is a recipe for her that is not too risky.

Utensils. 1. Pastry board and roller. 2. A fine sieve. 3. A basin. 4. A knife. It is also as well, as you are a mug, to have at hand a bowl of hot water in which to dip your fingers should you at the first attempt have made your dough too sticky and become attached to your surroundings.

Ingredients. 1. Eight ounces of flour—it can be plain, self-raising or half plain and half self-raising. 2. Two ounces of margarine and two ounces of lard, or if more convenient four ounces of margarine or even four ounces of lard, though personally I do not like this so much. 3. Pinch of salt. 4. A very small cup of cold water.

Procedure. Sieve the flour and salt into a basin —sieving always makes flour lighter. Mix in the fat with the tips of your fingers—this is, in my opinion, the most difficult part of the business, as it is also the most important. You must be very quick and light. Do not rub hard or use more than your finger-tips. The result should be a mass of crumbs. Stir the water into this with a knife (which is easier to use here than a spoon), then turn the resultant dough on to the pastry board, which you have already well floured. Roll out quickly, using the roller only in one direction, not to and fro, till the dough is of the required thickness.

If you are making a pie, remember to wet the edges of the pie dish, so that the crust sticks to it.

Your oven should be quick, and if you are making only small cases, they will be ready in ten minutes or so. A piecrust takes about half an hour. The baking is the process most likely to let you down, as it is largely invisible. You must not be continually opening the oven door, to see how things are getting on inside; so until someone invents an oven with a glass door—which to the lay mind does not seem much more difficult than inventing a bomb that travels at six thousand miles an hour through the stratosphere—the early stages of baking must remain as secret as those of gestation. For this reason it is as well not to attempt pastry unless you are unusually well off in the matter of fats.

Savories are much more economical than sweets, so I make them more often. They can easily be made out of any small remains, without serious inroads on more precious substances. Fish or liver chopped up small, bound with a little dried egg and seasoned with pepper and salt, with a dash of anchovy essence (if you have it) in the first case and a dash of chutney in the second, make pleasant little canapés on toast. American sardines are low on points and very good on toast, as are also canned herrings and pilchards. If you have artichokes, celery, leeks, or cauliflower, these are excellent when boiled and covered, after you have cut them up, with a white sauce to which you have added a tablespoon of grated cheese. You can also stuff tomatoes and onions with leftovers bound with dried egg.

This is at least one move in the direction of the good French custom of serving vegetables as a separate course. In England we are too much inclined to treat them as a mere accompaniment to more important matters, and as a result we often cook them badly. In big establishments they are commonly left to the kitchenmaid, and it used to be quite normal to find a skilled and experienced cook who served mushy sprouts and watery potatoes.

A cook once said to me, "Any fool can boil potatoes" —meaning that the parlormaid could do so on her (the cook's) evening out. As it happened, this cook herself could not produce boiled potatoes except as a soggy mess. She cooked them too long and too fast. They should be put (in their skins) in boiling, salted water and cooked without being allowed to "gallop" till nearly done, which will take from fifteen to twenty minutes. Then strain off the water, take off the skins and put the potatoes back in the saucepan with the lid on. Stand the pan on a warm part of the stove—but not on a hot plate or you will lose your saucepan—and let the potatoes cook in hot air for ten minutes longer. They will—or ought to—be beautifully floury.

A very appetizing way of cooking potatoes is to scoop potato balls out of two or three large potatoes with one of those weapons sold for the purpose. The balls should be cooked in a very little fat in a deep frying pan, with a saucepan lid fitted over it. Shake it from time to time to prevent them from sticking to the bottom, and every now and then turn them over with a fork. They take about twenty minutes to cook and should be golden brown all over. The lid on the frying pan is to prevent them from drying up or burning in the very small quantity of fat you can spare.

But potatoes are not a vegetable to be served separately. They are rightly an accompaniment to meat or fish or fowl. For a separate course you may use almost every other vegetable there is, but sprouts and cabbage require help of some kind if they are to stand alone. A little bacon is a great improver of both, so are a few chestnuts. Even elderly turnips can be made palatable by being diced and after cooking for thirty to forty minutes in boiling, salted water, covered with a white sauce, to the flour of which you have added a teaspoon of mustard powder.

Points for the mug to remember in cooking green vegetables are:—1. That they should always be cooked in fast-boiling salted water. 2. That on no account should soda be added to improve the color, as this also takes the flavor and goodness out of them. 3. That for the same reason they should not be "soaked" before cooking. (Wash them under the tap, after taking off the outer leaves.) 4. That they should not be cooked too long or in too much water—green vegetables should not be pulpy but slightly crunchy when they come to the table. It should not be possible to eat them without your teeth.

A pinch of sugar in the saucepan greatly improves the flavor of young carrots and young peas, and I always put sprig of mint into the water when cooking either peas or new potatoes. If you want to make a cauliflower more interesting, melt a walnut of margarine and stir in some dried bread crumbs, pouring the result over the vegetable just before serving. (This also goes for marrow.) If you can add a finely chopped hard-boiled egg, so much the better. Here too is a dodge for removing that abominable stink (I can find no calmer word) which proclaims to your family that cauliflower awaits them. I do not think you can be held guilty of wasting bread if you cut off half a slice of the crust, wrap it in a piece of muslin or a worn-out handkerchief and put it into the saucepan with the cauliflower. The characteristic reek will be removed as if by magic.

If you are serving vegetables as a separate course you will not naturally want to serve them with the main dish. Let this be accompanied by potatoes and a salad. A salad does not go well with made-up dishes, but it goes with very many more things than we ever serve it with in this country, where indeed it usually appears only as the accompaniment of cold food. Try it with any kind of roast meat—many of us used to eat it with roast chicken—or with a fried or grilled dish. A salad also can be switched round with your vegetables as a separate course, in which case you may enrich it with sundry cold remains of fish or meat or cooked vegetables. The dressing can either be the usual combination of oil (medicinal paraffin) and vinegar, or it may be an ersatz mayonnaise.

For the former, put a dessertspoon of vinegar into the bowl which you have already rubbed round with a slice of raw onion (or if you like it and have it, garlic), then add a pinch of salt, a shake of pepper, half a teaspoon of mustard powder and a teaspoon of sugar. Stir together and then put in your salad, which you should leave for twenty minutes or so to marinate. Add your oil just before serving—four tablespoons if it is real, not more than two if it isn't, and toss the whole thing thoroughly with a wooden spoon and fork. Some people like more vinegar, but I believe in the French saying—"a miser with the vinegar, a spendthrift with the oil, a maniac with the tossing."

Quite a passable substitute for mayonnaise can be made without eggs by making an ordinary white sauce with milk in which you have previously boiled an onion. Add pepper and salt and a teaspoon or less of mustard to the flour you stir into the margarine, and when the sauce is thick pour it into a small basin which you must put into a larger one of cold water, and stir it till it cools, or a skin will form. Not till it is quite cold can you add the vinegar without risk of curdling. I add only a tablespoon to half a pint of sauce, because we do not like vinegar, but most people would prefer at least twice this amount.

3.

NOW FOR SOME SHIFTS, SHAMS AND SWINDLES. So far we have considered only family meals, dishes that can be tried on the dog. But as the mug grows in experience and dexterity she will also probably grow in ambition and want to show off before a larger audience. Alternatively she may give way to despair and Spam; but I am calculating on her following the same course as I did, and, having fed her household for a week or two without catastrophe, become swollen up with surprise and pride and want to give a dinner party.

Mine was only a very modest one of four people altogether, and I think it would be wise not to increase your numbers too suddenly. If you normally cook only for yourself and your husband, the "twice two" sum will be quite difficult enough to start with. But if you are used to cooking for four people, then you need not be afraid of six or even eight.

There are one or two important considerations to bear in mind if you want to succeed in your object, which I assume is not merely to feed your guests, or even to give them a pleasant evening, but to make a good impression as a cook.

The first thing is not to attempt a meal which will involve you in working up to the last minute. You want to be standing there, calm, cool, clean and collected, to welcome your visitors, and you do not want to be running to and fro continually between the dining room and the kitchen.

I once read an article in a women's journal, which described in detail how dressing and making up could be fitted into the interstices of a three-course dinner. There was a definite point at which the cook left the soup and brushed her hair, another at which she left the main dish and finally fixed it. Her eye-black went on somewhere among the vegetables, her lipstick after she had tasted the sauce, and a lull after the sweet had gone into the oven allowed her to change her dress.

I can conceive no procedure more likely to ruin both the dinner and the morale (to say nothing of the appearance) of the hostess. The dinner, too, seemed to me badly chosen for a hostess cook, as it was of a fussy nature and hot throughout—even the sweet was hot, which seemed an unnecessary complication. A cold sweet can be prepared well beforehand and be off your mind during the main struggle. Indeed, if your first dinner party is given in summer, you might be wise to serve an entirely cold meal.

This sounds unenterprising and goes against custom, but it makes an ideal start for the green cook, as she can concentrate entirely on the dishes themselves, undisturbed by the time factor. This is much more important than you may think. Few of us realize that the most difficult thing in the world is to cook and serve a dinner of various courses absolutely to time. It is the acid test of efficiency, and I think I may say that the average professional cook avoids it.

From what I have observed in the past and experienced myself more recently I am pretty sure that the average professional cook has her whole dinner ready (excepting, of course, soufflés and such tricksy things) some little while before it is needed. By the time the soup is on the table, the joint or bird is dished up and keeping warm in the oven with its escorting dishes of vegetables and gravy. The pudding, if hot, is reposing in a *bain-marie*; if cold, it was probably made much earlier. I can remember my mother's struggles with an excellent but highly eccentric cook, who chose to get up at five and cook all the meals of the day before breakfast. I myself have often been greeted in the morning with such as, "I thought you might like a lemon sponge for dinner, so I've made one," or, "I've started jugging that hare for tonight—that's what smells so good."

The point of these maneuvers in each case was that the cook should be "beforehand with the world," which is more than excusable, even though I do not think she need have been quite so much beforehand. Experience had taught her to avoid like the plague that half hour of crisis in which everything seems to be requiring attention at once. A cook with a kitchenmaid is in easier circumstances, but a singlehanded cook has learned to dread the congestions of a critical moment, with their resulting dangers and delays; and if these are the tactics of an experienced professional, how much more necessary are they or something like them to the inexperienced amateur.

There is also the size of the stove to consider, for the modern, small electric or gas cooker often has not the cooking space for a large meal, if this is cooked all together; and in these times there is the further shortage of equipment—the same saucepan may have to do duty more than once. Altogether it is wise for the mug not to put herself into such a position.

She can of course serve a hot meal which has been cooked beforehand and requires only warming up. Long before the war a friend of mine who loved to give large dinner parties but could afford only one young, callow maid had evolved a most satisfactory technique by which she and the girl between them cooked the dinner in the morning, and then in the evening heated the various dishes in a *bain-marie*, from which the maid brought them to table. This of course limited the menu —anything roasted or fried or requiring a freshly cooked sauce or subtle last-minute touches had to be avoided—but the dinner was always very good indeed, unusual and well cooked, and gave the hostess and her assistant very little trouble.

We will consider a hot meal later, but I think the cold one is more agreeable and unusual as well as more easily prepared, since you will be involved in no cooking whatsoever at the time of your guests' arrival—everything will be ready in the dining room. I suggest the menu with which I made my own start.

Cold jellied soup
Mousse of chicken
Chocolate ice cream

Of course the whole thing is a swindle. Your jellied soup is not jellied with the richness of veal and chicken bones but with ordinary gelatine, your chicken is a rabbit and your cream is evaporated milk. But the difference between the dishes when made and their unattainable counterparts in the World of Ideas will not be nearly so great as you and your guests' pleasure in eating them and your ease in making and serving them. Incidentally the fuel controller ought to approve of your dinner party, for it involves very little fuel.

A genuine clear soup is one of the most difficult and extravagant dishes in the world. It demands a knuckle of veal, a shin of beef and the carcass of a chicken, several hours' simmering, frequent skimming and a final clearance with eggshells. So you must realize the economy of using instead only a dessertspoonful of meat essence, two onions, two carrots, a stick of celery, a bouquet of herbs and simmering these together for only half an hour.

Dissolve your meat essence—or a good vegetable essence will do as well—in about a quart of boiling water, then add the onions and carrots cut into slices, the bouquet of herbs and a few peppercorns. Simmer very gently and taste from time to time, for you do not want any one flavor to predominate; and before you have finished you may have to remove the herbs or the onions. Neither do you want the finished result to taste of meat essence. So taste carefully, removing vegetables or adding seasoning as required.

Meanwhile you will have dissolved a leaf of gelatine, which you will add to the soup before bringing it finally to the boil and pouring it into a wide flat dish or baking tin. Leave it in the larder to cool and set; it will hasten matters if you put it into the refrigerator but do not do so till it is cool. It ought not to set too hard—not like a jelly mold, but in a soft, blobby way. Then when it is ready and it suits you best, spoon it out into soup cups (this sort of soup must always be served in cups, not on plates) and return it to the refrigerator till the time comes to put it on the table.

The chicken mousse requires a cooked rabbit (we always have a meal off ours first, but your numbers may not allow this), a breakfast cup of milk, a teacup of evaporated milk, a small onion, peppercorns, a bay leaf, a leaf of gelatine, a dessertspoonful of flour, half an ounce of margarine, and seasoning.

The first and most laborious thing to do is to take your rabbit meat off the bones and put it through the mincer *twice*. This is essential, as the meat should be very fine and soft—in fact I sometimes also beat it up in a pestle and mortar. Meanwhile you will boil your milk very slowly, over a low heat, in a saucepan which also contains the onion, bay leaf and peppercorns. When this is ready make a white sauce by melting the margarine in another saucepan, stirring in the flour till you have made a smooth, thick cream (or *roux* as it is technically called) and then adding the strained milk gradually, stirring till your sauce is thick.

Add the sauce to the minced rabbit, and let the whole thing simmer very, very slowly for about half an hour.

During this time you can dissolve your gelatine and whip your evaporated milk. Pour the latter into a basin big enough to contain the entire mousse and whip it with an egg-whisk until it looks like thick cream. Some people say it is more satisfactory if you boil the milk first by standing the tin in a saucepan of boiling water, and then when it is cool put it in the icebox for several hours; but though I have tried this method I have not found that it makes any appreciable difference and it certainly adds to the toils of the cook.

Remember that your cream will not remain creamy indefinitely, so you should not whip it till you are ready to use it, which will be when you have added the gelatine to the simmering rabbit and brought the whole thing to the boil. Then pour it very slowly and gradually into the "cream," stirring the whole time; see that the seasoning is right and pour into a soufflé dish. When the mousse is set, cover the top with chopped parsley—of course the ideal is a top of aspic jelly, but that—like so many ideals—is probably beyond your attainment in a world of restrictive realities.

If you cannot get hold of a rabbit, this mousse may also be made of Spam, in which case, of course, it becomes a ham mousse.

For chocolate ice cream you require some more of the evaporated milk—probably the rest of the tin. You will also require for four people two heaped tablespoons of cocoa. I prefer mine unsweetened, as then I can regulate the amount of sweetness in the ice, which if made of sweetened cocoa is generally too sweet for my taste. But if you have a sweet tooth, sweetened cocoa certainly saves sugar and trouble. Dissolve your cocoa and sugar in a teacup of milk over a low heat, and stir till it boils into a thick, creamy paste. It should be just fluid enough to pour slowly into a pudding basin. Leave it there to cool.

In another basin you will have ready some whipped evaporated milk, as stiff as you can make it, in the proportions of two cupfuls of "cream" to one of chocolate. "Fold" the cream into the chocolate, that is mix them with a gentle dipping motion of your spoon which is not the same as stirring—not so rough. Add a pinch of salt, and if you like it, a teaspoon of vanilla essence; then pour the mixture into the ice container immediately under the freezing element of your refrigerator—having first removed, of course, the gadget which divides the ice into cubes. One container as a rule holds just enough ice cream for four people. You will already have made your refrigerator as cold as possible, for your ice should freeze quickly.

And now I fear that I am going to show myself as big a mug as you are. I confess that I am unable to tell you how long your mixture will take to freeze. Mine takes about four hours, but a friend's ices are ready in forty minutes. I do not know why this is and nobody has been able to tell me. The recipe book does not help, because it says only—"it all depends. . . ." Bear this in mind, however—the sweeter the mixture the longer it will take to freeze. Certain kinds of sweetened, condensed milk will not freeze at all. It is also important that you should dip the bottom of the container in water before you start freezing, as this greatly speeds up the process.

I recommend Mrs. Mugg to start freezing her mixture about three o'clock, if she wants to take it out at eight. Time does not add to her labors, because in this method there is no stirring to do. Just leave the thing to freeze. You can test it from time to time with the tip of your finger, and if you find it is growing too hard, you can raise the temperature of the refrigerator. Personally I found my ice a little on the soft side after four hours. But here is another mystery. The next time I made the dish I put it in two hours earlier and it was softer still. I am ashamed to say that I cannot even guess the reason, for we have entered those realms of mechanical science in which I am a child. All I can suggest is that some day before the party you should have a dress rehearsal, in which you will discover the peculiarities of your refrigerator.

Of course it is possible that after you have read this you may decide not to have an ice at all. In that case I suggest a fruit salad as less likely to destroy your peace of mind. It is not a very exciting or original dish, but if you keep it a few hours on ice it will be nearly as refreshing as an ice cream, and you will already have excited your friends enough with your cold consommé and chicken mousse. It also has the moral advantage of being the only dish on the menu which is not a sham and an outrage on orthodox cookery.

But, the mug protests, though this may do all very well for a summer meal, I do not want to chill and freeze my friends in winter. I *must* have a hot dinner that I can prepare easily. Such undoubtedly exist. They do, and here is one of them—or rather, two courses of it, for I still think a hot sweet an unnecessary complication.

First for the soup. Make it in exactly the same way as you made the jellied soup, but without the gelatine. A spoonful of wine is a sensational improvement. You will also make it extremely interesting if, much earlier in the day, you beat up the yolk of an egg (or a dried egg reconstituted) in a tablespoonful of milk and pour it into a greased and covered pipkin, to stand in a saucepan of boiling water. Keep the water simmering till the egg has solidified to the consistency of custard, then let it cool and turn it out before cutting it up into small pieces which you drop into the soup just before it is ready to serve.

After the soup you had better have a casserole dish of some sort, a jointed bird or rabbit, or a few cutlets. Your choice (or luck) should be browned first in a little fat. Take the pieces out and then in the same fat fry a medium-sized onion cut in slices. Pour off any fat that is left and put back the meat, on a bed of vegetables—carrots, leeks, turnip, whatsoever you happen to have, all sliced up. Add a herbal bouquet and some seasoning and cover the lot with stock or water and—most important of all—the lid. Bring slowly to the boil and then simmer till the meat is tender, which will take at least an hour.

Remember that the excellence of a casserole depends on the flavoring, so taste yours from time to time, and make small improvements such as a dash of ketchup or a dreg of wine or even a dreg of beer. I have known a stew to be greatly improved by a dessertspoonful of treacle. But do not be too enterprising and add a number of flavorings—just one of these will be enough; and remember that there should be no definite single taste —only a combined effect in which only a connoisseur could distinguish the various ingredients.

When your meat is tender, take it out and keep it hot while you strain off the liquor from the vegetables. Then melt a small piece of fat in the saucepan and stir in a tablespoonful of flour; pour back the liquor gradually, stirring all the while, till your gravy is thick. You may add a dash of browning if you want to darken it, but this, strictly speaking, should not be required if you have made your sauce properly. In a brown sauce you do not, as you do at all costs in making a white one, avoid browning the flour; on the contrary, you should stir it till it has browned in the fat. But for the beginner this sometimes results (especially if your saucepan is war-weary) in burning. So unless you have already proved your dexterity, it is best to stir more briefly and use an artificial coloring.

Ideally, too, this dish should be cooked in the oven and served in the casserole it is cooked in. But as on this occasion you will not require the oven for anything else, it is more economical to cook it on the top of the stove if you cook by gas or electricity, and in any case a casserole in the oven is more difficult to watch over and taste from than a saucepan on the top of the stove. So for the beginner, cooking for her first dinner party, it is the wiser course to have everything under her eye and in reach of her tongue.

With the casserole you will serve vegetables as with the cold chicken mousse you served a salad. The vegetables under the meat will now exist only as flavoring, so it will be necessary to serve others as an accompaniment.

This is another reason for avoiding a hot dinner at your first party, for vegetables should be eaten directly they are cooked. The best way out of the difficulty would be to cook them at the last minute, after you are dressed, and then leave them in a *bain-marie*—that is in a covered, fireproof basin or vegetable dish placed over a saucepan of boiling water, which should be allowed to simmer over a low heat till the time of dishing up arrives. This method keeps food hot without cooking it further or letting it dry up as it would if kept in the oven; but it is a process better suited to sauces, gravies and stews than to vegetables, so I hope your friends will not protract it unduly by lingering over their drinks.

4.

THESE TWO MENUS, THE COLD AND THE HOT, ARE OF course not the only ones the mug can serve her guests. I give them as specimens of what can be achieved and of ways of achieving it. Here are a half dozen more, not necessarily for parties, which can be easily prepared out of ingredients not too difficult to obtain, especially by those living in the country. For these menus I supply no directions, nor do I suggest garnishes, which must depend on taste and circumstances.

Tomato and onion soup (soup *aux noces*)
Slices of veal, bread crumbed and fried, served with
    chopped olives and hard-boiled egg
        (A fake of filet de veau viennoise)
Coffee ice cream

Cucumber soup
Risotto
Doucegrove toast (small rounds of fried bread with
    sweet chutney and chopped walnuts)

Celery boats (short lengths of celery filled with
    melted cheese)

Fish poached in milk with tomatoes and onions
Apple snow

Brownbread soup
Mackerel (tinned) with fennel sauce
Gooseberry jelly

Hollandaise soup
Salmi of rabbit with mushrooms
Orange ice cream

Eggs *en cocotte* (with the top of the milk)
Baked beans *à la bretonne*
Lemon curd tartlets

Leek and oatmeal soup
Mayonnaise of pilchards and corn salad
Jam omelette

And here are twenty-five ways of cooking rabbit. 1. Baked and stuffed (with bread sauce). 2. Fried on toast (when very young). 3. Fried with *sauce piquante*. 4. Stewed in a little wine. 5. With oatmeal and shallots. 6. With sweet corn. 7. With brown sauce and prunes. 8. With mushrooms or mushroom sauce. 9. With paprika sauce. 10. With hollandaise sauce. 11. With *Béchamel* sauce. 12. With Normandy sauce. 13. *à la marengo*, with olives and tomatoes. 14. As cold chicken soufflé. 15. As chicken galantine. 16. As stuffing for a cabbage. 17. As *rissoles*. 18. In a steamed mold. 19. Diced in a jellied mold. 20. In a pie. 21. As potted meat for sandwiches. 22. With an orange (juice and grated rind) and button onions. 23. With a very ritzy sauce made of margarine, flour, rabbit liquor, milk, cheese, white wine and the beaten *white* of an egg. 24. Curried. 25. In a border of rice cooked with a sprig of rosemary.

In securing raw materials for your kitchen I suggest that you do not cling too closely to that idealized picture of yourself in which you hope your butcher has framed you. I once took back two small kidneys which mine had sent me very much more than once too often.

"Haven't you anything else in the way of offal?"

"No, madam, absolutely nothing but these two beautiful English kidneys."

"Yes, I know they're beautiful, and it was very kind of you to send them. But I had them last week too (and how many more weeks?) And my husband doesn't eat them."

This for some reason provoked universal merriment.

I saw myself going sadly home with my two kidneys, when my eyes suddenly fell upon an object—a profile—lying on the slab.

"Haven't you got a pig's face?"

A silence that could be heard, and then a shocked voice—

"Yes, madam, *but we never thought you ate that sort of thing.*"

That sort of remark always challenges me.

"Oh, yes, I do," I said briskly, though I was beginning to feel doubtful in view of the reverse side of the profile which had now been displayed.

I had accepted the butcher's challenge and he now accepted mine. He threw in a calf's foot, and I fled for fear that he might also add pigs' trotters and a calf's head. My tiny parcel of decent offal had been exchanged for an armful of unsightly horror and I could not help realizing that the seven or eight minutes required to grill a kidney had probably also been exchanged for as many hours.

Actually that pig's face and calf's foot kept me busy for a whole weekend before they finally became two molds of brawn, a mold of calf's foot jelly, a huge basin of stock, and a jar of lard. They fed not only my family but my cat, my hens, and in final solution a mob of wild birds seeking food in a world of snow.

But I cannot bear to think of my butcher's shattered illusions as to what lady novelists eat.

5.

IT IS NOW TIME FOR MRS. MUGG AND MYSELF TO COME out of our conference and return to any company that remains. I think I have written enough to show that I am wise not to write any more, and also to suggest the kind of cookery book required for real ignorant mugs who do not know the difference between a panada and a pattypan, a *roux* and a stew.

It is not likely that there will be many of these in future, because I imagine that hard pressure of circumstances will prevent any girl from being brought up as I was, without the smallest knowledge of domestic matters. But it is always possible that some may prefer to teach themselves to being taught by others, and for such a primer is necessary. But let it be a real primer, written on the virgin slate of the reader's ignorance. Let it also, while adapting itself to such difficulties and scarcities as are likely to remain, discourage the spirit of defeatism which has invaded some of our kitchens.

Not long ago I cooked a pound of sprats most deliciously in seasoned flour and a nut of fat. I had previously been told by a professional cook that this was impossible "as sprats require deep frying." They do not, of course, being an oily fish, and even Mrs. Beeton suggests no more than half an ounce of lard. But if I had not been my own cook I should have had to go without a fish which I like even better than oysters.

The other side of defeatism is represented by a friend to whom I told the story.

"Oh, but," she exclaimed eagerly, "you don't have to use fat at all. You can boil them in just a little salted water."

I asked her: "But do they taste as good?"—and she looked blank.

She had already told me that she had "discovered" a way of making vegetable soup without using margarine, and it did not seem to occur to her that such an omission would spoil the flavor. Nor, I imagine, would she think it any serious drawback if it did.

The trouble is, of course, that at the present time there are many people cooking to whom food means nothing except nourishment—an idea which I fear has been encouraged in certain official quarters. I am all on the side of those who do not mind losing a vitamin or two if thereby they enhance the pleasantness of a meal. When I was a child I was never made to eat anything repulsive to me—unlike other children of my acquaintance who often had rejected food literally forced down their throats. My father, a doctor of the old school, believed that food, in order to be satisfactorily digested, should be enjoyed, as such enjoyment stimulated the digestive juices of the mouth and stomach, whereas its absence inhibited them. In other, more familiar, words, "A bit of what you fancy does you good." Some of our fancies may be difficult to materialize in lean times, but they are not all necessarily unattainable, at least with a little contrivance, and a good cook should take pleasure in accepting the challenge flung down by adversity.

I have often wondered what qualities go to make a good cook. At one time I thought it was intelligence, but I have revised that opinion in view of the fact that one of my best cooks was also the stupidest. Moreover, I have myself cooked two very successful meals when my brain was not functioning at all—once owing to an attack of asthma and once owing to a "saturation" bombardment of which the B.B.C. used elegantly to call missiles.

Is it intuition, then?—a sort of sense?—part of the animal's instinct to feed itself? I do not believe it—I have eaten too many hard-boiled eggs, underdone joints and burnt cakes, attributable to the cook's using her instinct in preference to less romantic methods of calculation. Is it a personal appreciation of good food? Again I am obliged to say No, though in this case I should have preferred to say Yes. For I have had a really first-class cook who herself ate nothing but steamed fish, milk and eggs, owing to digestive weakness. She

·[118]·

made the most delicious dishes which she never even tasted, and took endless trouble to produce what to her would have meant nothing but dyspepsia. She was able to cook when she herself was feeling very ill, and seemed to take a real pleasure and pride in her achievements.

My conclusion, therefore, is that cooking is a gift and the good cook as mysterious and unpredictable an artist as the good painter or the good poet, though mercifully not so rare. Cooking is an art which, like so many others, has become a trade. Like so many others it has fallen into the wrong hands and been both exploited and neglected. But as adversity often invigorates art that had been debilitated by a commercial civilization, so perhaps struggle and scarcity, and the introduction of new blood into the kitchen, in the shape of the mistress of the house, may give our English cooking a chance which it has not had since the eighteenth century.

Part IV
Episodic

1.

ON ENTERING INTO NEW RELATIONS WITH THE KITCHEN one also enters into new relations with the cat. One sees him as it were in his shirt sleeves, no longer seeking to impress. My present view of him would be a variation of the German *Strassengel, Hausteufel*. He may indeed be an angel in the drawing room—aloof, mysterious, communing with the Unseen; but in the kitchen he is nothing but a devil, seeking what he may devour and the father of lies—never before have I had it shown me so clearly that an animal can lie. A dog-loving friend once boasted that her pet "actually came to me and told me as plain as any words that he hadn't had his dinner." My cat has often told me the same story equally plainly, when, unknown to me, he had just indulged in a large meal, or has a rabbit in store behind the radiator, or even—horrible to relate—a bird under the sofa.

Dog lovers are a credulous, emotional race; a little flattery from the faithful friend and he is faultless. Cat lovers, on the other hand, are cynical, and well aware of the moral deficiencies of the beloved. The only quality which they will not hear denied is his intelligence. This quality has never been given its due by those who expect an animal's intelligence to work on the same lines as their own. In fact I believe it has been formally "disproved" by a scientist whose name I very properly forget, who shut up a cat in a box with some simple contraption for its exit which it failed to use. At least that was his account of the experiment; anyone who understood cats would have said "refused" to use. The point is that the cat realized he was being exploited, and having no doglike wish to ingratiate himself, refused to collaborate. He did not choose to come out of that box, or he would have done so. Those who doubt this statement have only to try by any method short of physical violence, to keep a cat in some place he wishes to leave or out of some place he wishes to enter.

I have at the moment two cats—Tuesday and Nikolous Ridikulous. They are both in a true sense kitchen cats, preferring the hot-water pipes that run under the sink to any softer couch in upholstered surroundings. All my cats, I suppose, have had a separate kitchen life in which I had little share, but these appear to have no other existence. Nikolous occasionally pursues the tea-trolley into the sitting room and enjoys there a saucer of the milk he has refused in the kitchen, but that is his only aspiration to gentility.

Tuesday is supposedly the garden cat, though he spends—in winter at least—some fourteen hours of the twenty-four curled up in a basket under the kitchen cupboard. He was acquired in response to a sudden cry from Joe Boorman the gardener that he "wanted a cat that earned its living"—a cry prompted by my Persian cat's benevolent habit of bringing small rabbits into the kitchen garden and depositing them there uninjured to grow fat in the cabbage bed.

So Tuesday came, but he has never earned his living. In summer he was reported to "feed he's self," but I now know well that he doesn't. He is huge and fat and lazy, a beautiful tabby, with haunting eyes, green as grapes and bright as Neon lights. Unfortunately he has been brought up to be rough, and scratches and bites the unwary in the spirit of painful play. When we had servants he was kept out of the house, but he infiltrated himself soon after their departure and now would be more difficult to dislodge than my husband.

Nikolous is the official house cat, but greatly inferior to Tuesday in appearance and breeding. He is a mean-looking tabby, with hazel eyes, a white vest, white spats and torn white gloves. He has a nervous, fussy, ingratiating manner, which irritates me intensely. Mr. T. S. Eliot would classify him in his *Book of Practical Cats* as a Rum-Tum Tugger; for—

> When you let him in, then he wants to be out;
> He's always on the wrong side of every door,
> And as soon as he's at home, then he'd like to get about . . .
> . . . he'll leap on your lap in the middle of your sewing.

He is always restless, always fussing; unless he is eating or sleeping he never sits still. But I cannot complain, for I acquired him definitely as a cure for a cat love which I had come to realize was reaching pathological proportions. His full title is Nikolous Ridikulous, the Cat to End All Cats.

I am a hereditary cat lover, for I can remember as a child my mother's deep addiction and its recognition by the series of family cats, who loved her and her only, in spite of my wooing. It was not till I married and had a cat of my own that I knew the joy of coming first in feline affections. John Henry (named after a radio star popular in the days of the earphone and the cat's whisker) was given me as a wedding present and lived the first five years of his life in London. He was a magnificent long-haired blue, with a huge ruff and voluminous plus fours. But his eyes were "wrong"—they were topaz instead of amber, a glorious gold like honey in sunshine. He had a huge head, housing a master brain. No scientist could have detained him in a box for a single unwilling moment.

As soon as he had grown tall enough to reach the handle he would open the door of any room in our flat. It was impossible to keep him out of the dining room during a dinner party, and he loved parties. He would march round the table like a mannequin, displaying his fur coat—I cannot deny that he was inordinately vain—and maintain his social equality by accepting trifles from the diners' plates.

This was a purely social gesture, for he himself had already dined and would have been affronted rather than gratified by the offering of the same food on a plate on the floor. When in his last illness he refused his ordinary meals he could still be tempted at our table; and I remember my husband taking out the car and driving three miles to the village shop because I had announced that Johnny had eaten a fish-paste sandwich and we had no more fish-paste in the house.

When he came to us I still knew very little about cats, though I had had some sort of relationship with them all my life. I made one or two very silly mistakes; for instance, when we moved from our flat in Holland Park to a house in Hereford Square, I was still far enough under the delusion that "cats prefer places to people" to arrange to leave John Henry behind, in charge of the porter and his wife, while the move was in progress. The very next day I had to go back to coax him out of a tree into which he had climbed and where he had insisted on remaining ever since our departure. He refused all accommodation in our empty flat or in the porter's basement. There was nothing to do but have him shut up at the vet's till we were established in our new home.

Here he settled down very happily, taking full advantage of the opportunities provided by a balcony which spanned the frontage of at least six houses. Obstacles had been set up to prevent human progress, but nothing that need deter a cat. In an incredibly short time John Henry had visited all our neighbors, inspected their houses from attic to basement and terrorized their dogs. He had a formidable manner with dogs, who, for the most part, prudently refused his challenges to combat. He himself was absolutely fearless and I once had to snatch him out of reach of an airedale-police dog who seemed more likely than others to take him on.

Toward our own dog, a highly intelligent, highly

hysterical little dachshund, he was kindness itself—kindness and firmness, for when Jimmy kept us awake at night with his barking we had only to shut him into the kitchen with Johnny to obtain complete silence and good behavior. Jimmy had sometimes, however, a very disrespectful way of treating his superior in age and wisdom; he would run underneath him on his short legs, and then hump his back so that the cat was swept off the ground and a situation created rather like that in which a small urchin on roller skates runs between the legs of an archbishop.

I could understand the temptation, for John Henry was, at times, preposterously majestical; I can similarly understand the mockery and derision in which Jimmy indulged when Johnny came home one day from the vet's with most of his fur clipped off. But poor Johnny could not understand it at all and brooded so deeply on his humiliation that the vet had to be called in again for what he told me was in fact a nervous breakdown. The cat jumped over the moon because he could not endure being laughed at—and the little dog laughed to see such sport.

John Henry bore him no ill will, however. When he had recovered his mental balance they played together as happily as ever and slept in each other's arms. Johnny loved to give presents to Jimmy. I have watched him climb to the topmost shelf of the larder, extract with infinite fastidiousness a piece of meat from a steak and kidney pie and carry it to the dog. He also dispensed charity; for while refusing to let the cook's cat emerge from the basement and treating with the utmost grief and resentment any unfaithfulness I might be guilty of with other cats, he always allowed a genuine stray to come into the house, eat its fill and have a good sleep in front of the fire before he chased it away. After we had moved into the country, for weeks he gave hospitality to a seedy derelict from the woods, though always keeping a careful watch while it was about, very much after the style of a charitable householder feeding a tramp.

That move into the country was a great and terrible disruption of his life, though he adapted himself to it more easily than I had expected. For five years he had been a London cat, taking his pleasure in houses and back yards, exercising his hunting instinct deplorably in the larder. Moreover we were to be six months without a home, visiting Italy and then settling in rooms near the farmhouse that was being rebuilt. Obviously he could not spend all that time incarcerated at the vet's, nor with us on our travels; for I did not know then that cats—or perhaps I should say some cats—can be trained as traveling companions and that we could at least have had him with us in our rooms in the country.

The solution of the problem was his establishment in a magnificent cats' hotel, where he had a room to himself with three windows facing south, and every luxury of bed and board. I felt it was the best and the least I could do for him. He would not be happy, but would have his comforts and a measure of exercise and freedom; moreover, a friend of mine and his who lived near undertook to visit him.

He remained at his hotel for over nine months and when I went to fetch him away I was told so firmly by all my friends that he would have forgotten me that I was almost fool enough to believe them. The idea, or rather insult, perished in the first moments of reunion —in the greeting ecstasy of his purrs, and in the complete readiness with which he adapted himself to his new life.

For two days he occupied a vantage point at the corner of the stairs, from which he could see both up and down, after which he went about the house—and more remarkably the fields and garden—with the same confidence that he had roamed the back yards of South Kensington. He never ventured far into the woods which crowd right up to the back of our house and have been the undoing of many cats, but he soon showed himself an enthusiastic hunter of bigger game than could be found in the larder.

Unfortunately (except for his victims) he did not hunt to kill. We were in those days, prodigiously plagued with rabbits, which invaded our garden in spite of a Maginot line of barbed wire dug deep into the ground. Johnny, who must have had an inordinately gentle mouth, would assist the enemy by bringing him in and depositing him, startled but unhurt, in the midst of our choicest vegetables and flowers. Hence the creation of the office of garden cat.

This was not filled, however, until after his death. He would have resented it too deeply. I once in a moment of folly introduced another cat, but his sojourn was brief. I cannot now think how I came to be so stupid, but I told myself at the time that Johnny was growing old and needed young life and companionship —a trick of reasoning my mind may have imposed on me to soften the thought of his death, which was at this time drawing within measurable expectation.

The new kitten was to be a continuation of himself, a long-haired blue of high lineage and noble intelligence, trained, perhaps I hoped, in feline virtue by the paragon he was to succeed. But Johnny's first reaction to his own immortality in my affections was to take my hand in his teeth and roll his eyes at me in tigerish threat, as if to say, "I am so angry I could crack your bones." He did this to me only twice in his life and the second time it was for so flimsy a reason—some passing loss of temper during one of his many combings—that he immediately saw his error and apologized. But he did not apologize this first time. He withdrew himself.

For days he would hardly look at me. Like most animals he vented his jealous rage on the beloved rather than on the rival. He could have chewed the kitten to mince, but he never attempted to injure it, though once in a sudden fit of exasperation he hit it slightly but angrily on the head, making at the same time a cross, irritable, peevish noise, quite unlike anything in his usual vocabulary. He hated it and shunned it, and the kitten mocked him and pursued him, evidently enjoying some secret animal privilege of youth. It took possession, one after the other, of all the rooms in the house and each room it occupied Johnny would never re-enter.

In the end I could endure the situation no longer. My friends all insisted blithely that it would not last, that soon the two cats would be inseparable buddies, and I must steel my heart to the transition period. But when three weeks had passed without any amiable conclusion of the matter I decided to end my old friend's misery. For he undoubtedly was miserable, and in some definite way humiliated. I could not allow it to be. The kitten was attractive—we had called him Robert Douce, after the French emigrant who started the iron industry in this part of Sussex and left his name to all the Douches, Dowses and Doucegroves of the neighborhood. Robert Douce was on points a better cat than Johnny— his nose was shorter and his forehead bumpier, and his eyes were a smoky amber. He was also an intelligent and affectionate, if slightly malicious, little animal. But he had no real claims on me, no history of friendship, and I could not allow him to make a moping, fasting misery of Johnny's life. So I gave him to a cat-loving friend.

There were some curious manifestations on the day of his departure, for both cats seemed, mysteriously, to know what was intended. There had been nothing whatever done that might apprise them of it—no changes or preparations, no visit of inspection from the future owner. But when the time came to find Robert Douce for his journey to his new home, he had disappeared. Normally he was always close at hand, maintaining his territorial claims in the house, but this afternoon he had hidden himself in the garden. When at last we tracked him he ran away, when at last we caught him he scratched and fought. I had intended to hold him on my lap for the brief journey, for he "traveled" exceedingly well, but it was impossible to hold this struggling mass of wires and we had to put him in a box.

To see one's enemy carried out of the house, shut up in a box with holes bored in the lid, is a triumph only slightly inferior—if it is inferior—to seeing him carried out in his coffin. I am glad that Johnny enjoyed it, as he had intended. For when we came out to the car, there he was established in a door-side flower bed waiting to see his rival off the premises. As soon as we had gone he re-entered the house, ate the kitten's dinner as well as his own, and settled down comfortably to sleep. He obviously knew as well as we did that Robert would not come back. But how did he know?

I have asked this question on other occasions. How did he know, that morning we set out for the United States, that we were leaving him for longer than the usual brief absence? He had always resented our departure, but this time he showed actual grief, sitting huddled in plaintive misery, every now and then emitting a sorrowful cry, and finally pursuing the car as far as the end of the garden. How did he know that the stray cat he allowed into the house was dead and would come no more, so that he could relax his vigil in the hall o' nights and sleep peacefully in the sitting room as of old? We ourselves did not know till two days after we had observed the end of his alarms.

It seems obvious that animals have means of communication which we have lost with the acquirement of speech, but this foreknowledge suggests something more mysterious, though probably of the same nature. One meets it occasionally in human beings, who often regard it as a distinction, a mark of superiority if not of divine favor; whereas it is more likely to be a throwback to earlier, superseded conditions. Certainly it is not necessarily supernatural, though like all natural qualities it is capable of becoming so.

After the rout of Robert Douce, John Henry's life flowed on peacefully for some years. He had established it on exactly the lines he wanted. Though the heavy wooden latches of the country doors would not allow him to roam the house with the freedom he had enjoyed in London, he had immediately on arrival discovered how to slide open the service hatch, and would burst through this with a furious face and a noise like thunder if anyone attempted to imprison him on the wrong side of it.

At night he had the freedom of the house and garden; for a small window was left open for him to go in and out of, and often in the early hours of dawn I have wakened to his low hunting cry, as he went forth into the dusk of his outdoor estate. He could be trusted not to interfere with our chicken farm, as the only animal I have ever seen him show any fear of was a hen. My mind holds a shocking picture of a huge cat cowering in a ditch before a very small but very angry mother of ten chicks. But as he saw me witness this humiliation, it may have been pride as much as fear that made him thenceforward very distant in his attitude toward all poultry—except, of course, in their proper place on the dish.

Cattle and sheep he almost ignored. He evidently had no great opinion of them, and I have another, compensatingly heroic picture of him walking sedately on the edge of a field, indifferent to the fact that he was being followed by a herd of young steers. I was some little way off and a good deal alarmed. I feared that they would attack him, thinking he was dog—a pardonable mistake on their part, as it had been made more than once by human beings. He took not the slightest notice of them until they suddenly ran at him with their heads down. I screamed, but all the cat did was to turn round and glare at them with all the light in his yellow eyes. The herd stopped, swung their heads and lumbered off, while John Henry walked on calmly till he reached the hole in the hedge he wished to enter—not once did he look back.

But this good life must end; and it ended in the way it ends for many long-haired cats, who when washing

·[129]·

swallow quantities of their exaggeratedly thick fur. In his youth and middle-age this swallowing had been rectified every ten days or so by the regurgitation of a neat cigar—which became a familiar object on our lawn and an occasional one on our carpets. But old age made this process more difficult and infrequent, and in the end it stopped altogether, with the result that internal passages became blocked and that most perfect machine, a cat's body, lost its efficiency. All that a skillful vet could do was done, but when he had not eaten for several days and was growing hourly weaker it seemed both cruel and useless to do more. . . .

I had meant to carry on his history to its last moments, to that very last moment when he accepted death with the same dignity and benignity that he had accepted life. But these things are too painful to write about even now, after eight years. So I skip some hours and end with a posthumous picture of myself on Romney Marsh, to which some mysterious impulse always urges me in moments of grief but from which I have never had any comfort. I see the car halted in the midst of a panting flock of sheep, the flies are thick above them, rising from their unshorn fleeces, and my heart is sick with a pity that tears and cries.

2.

THE DEATH OF A BELOVED ANIMAL HITS ONE OVER the heart in much the same way as the death of a beloved human being, and though in the latter case the intellectual sense of loss is infinitely greater it is, at the moment anyway, relieved by a multitude of consolations and distractions which are absent when an animal dies. Our friends write, so generously that we are taken out of ourselves in response both emotional and literal, and there are endless technical matters to be considered with the law and the church, to say nothing of such domestic preoccupations as the visits of more relatives than the house will hold. There is also the spotlight of local sympathy as we play our small part on the stage of human sorrow—"Poor woman, she has lost her father—her mother—her husband—her brother—her sister. . . ." But who shall say, "Poor woman, she has lost her cat"? Who but the few and most elect will write a letter of sympathy? As for the law and the church, our beloved had nothing to leave us but his memory and we ourselves can dig his shallow grave among the poplars and plant a rosemary bush thereon.

In my own case there is a deprivation which I imagine does not affect either those who do not believe in human immortality or those who do believe in the immortality of animals. Until Johnny died no bereavement had found me except as one convinced not only of the loved one's survival but also of my own contribution toward what might be called the amenities of that survival. My loved ones in their eternity depended on me more than ever, and my whole being, captained by grief had marched to their assistance in prayer and sacrifice. Now all values are suddenly changed; my grief is helpless and in some way ashamed. I know what has been my own opinion of those who allow their hearts to be broken by the death of an animal.

I must be careful what I write here, for I touch a complex widespread throughout this nation. Most of us are not quite normal on the subject of animals. We have exaggerated loves and likings and exaggerated fears. On one side there are those who love their dog better than their neighbor or themselves, on the other those who could vomit—and sometimes do—at the sight of a spider or a cockroach, or even, strange as it may seem, a bird. I have feelings on both sides, but my mind—dare I say so?—is uncorrupted. I am a cat-addict, but one at this moment zealously engaged in a cure; I am terrified of spiders, black beetles, centipedes and such, but though here I have not yet had the moral strength to cure myself, I freely acknowledge that I am a fool. May I give

·[131]·

myself full marks mentally if I claim only five out of ten morally and nought out of ten emotionally?

The only occasion on which my husband challenged controversy in an otherwise blameless sequence of Anglican sermons was when he cast doubts on animal survival. Immediately his post became a variation on the theme: "I could not be happy in heaven without dear Fido." Such statements always prompt me to the question "What exactly do you mean by heaven?" Obviously if you mean, as I imagine most people mean who say this sort of thing, an infinite continuation of your present life under infinitely preferable conditions, there is no reason on earth why dear Fido should not share your bliss. He is just as capable of appreciating an endless good time as you are—in fact, more so, because he is not so likely to be bored by it in the long (very long) run.

But if, on the other hand, eternity is not just mere endlessness but the sum total of time and space, and if heaven is not mere earth but the Vision of God, I am not so sure of dear Fido's position. I know that Kipling in a late, rather sad little poem, proclaimed his hope of a happy reunion with his dead Aberdeen terrier, of being greeted by a low, dark, hairy body rushing out from "underneath the throne of Grace." It is a pretty fancy, and of course I should like to have a similar fancy as to my Persian cat, though I am quite sure that if there is a throne about my Johnny will not be *underneath* it (he had a technique of dislodgment by which he would eventually usurp the place of even the most firmly established sitters). But I cannot quite square the idea with what I take to be the essential nature of a cat, even of an exceptionally gifted and intelligent cat.

I do not think that my position as a Roman Catholic makes any difference here. I have never, when adhering to any other system of belief or unbelief, believed in the survival of animals. The Church does not formally and officially forbid the notion, though there is certainly nothing in her philosophy to encourage it, and I imagine that her theologians would deny it. Nor is it any part of the controversy as to whether animals have or have not souls. According to the teaching of St. Thomas Aquinas all animals have souls—necessarily, since the soul is the "form" of the body—but these souls are not like human souls, immortal. There is nothing inherently immortal about a soul, and the human soul is immortal only because it is made in the image of God.

An animal soul exists entirely in the order of nature —it obeys only natural laws; we see in it none of that tension between nature and supernature, body and spirit, which is characteristic of our own position, nor has it any of that sad knowledge of good and evil which has made us "as gods." Presumably that knowledge is not essential to immortality; but surely the capacity for it is—as is also the capacity for abstract thinking as distinct from the mere association of ideas. An animal presumably "thinks" in images, in intuitions and automatic associations, just as he acts according to inspirations that are instinctive and reflex. It is true that a great many people think and act in the same way. But at least anyone who is not mentally defective is capable at moments of some sort of abstract reflection of generalizations, of deductions, of reasonings, and anyone who is not a moral imbecile has an idea of right and wrong based on something less earthly than necessity or even the approval of those we love.

The trouble is that our conceptions of the spiritual often remain much as they were in childhood, when we went so very much further than orthodoxy and pictured Mrs. Brown rising from the dead not only in her flesh, but in her mantle and beaded bonnet. We saw her projected into a world which was very like this, except that it was perfectly agreeable and went on forever, and also had a soothing, not too aggressive religious atmosphere. We hoped to go there ourselves one day and felt rather depressed at the thought of having to meet Mrs. Brown.

I honestly think that this idea of heaven remains with many adults all their lives. In a recent symposium, *In Search of Faith,** Mr. George Bernard Shaw states: "I not only do not believe in personal immortality: I abhor it. My self-love does not make me so mad as to endure the thought of my living for ever: only a child incapable of comprehending eternity could face such a horror." And only a great man whose spiritual education had stopped short in childhood could hold such a conception of eternity. Of course Mr. Shaw may be doing here what he so often does so well—gamboling; but the idea of eternity as synonymous with endless time is widespread enough to show that there must be something wrong with our normal methods of acquiring religious knowledge.

It is possible that recent scientific and pseudo-scientific conjectures on time—clock time, absolute time, space time, all sorts of time—will induce the intelligent to pay more attention to ideas that hitherto they have dismissed as childish. Even the term "everlasting" may no longer horrify with its suggestion of an endless succession of nights and days. Einstein may persuade those who have been unconvinced by Christ. By this I mean only that the situation may become scientifically respectable, for I do not share the optimism of those who look to science for some ultimate "proof" of their hopes. Science has a different job to do, a job which involves the discipline of faith rather than its relaxation. I for one never expect to see it give any explanation of reality; I look rather to reality to give an explanation of science. *Mirabilis facta est scientia tua.*

But let us return to Mrs. Brown, and let me here exercise that freedom of conjecture in matters undefined which is one of the sports of Catholic security. Let me conjecture about eternity as I conjectured in another book about certain characters in Jane Austen's novels, attaching exactly the same weight to my conjectures in one case as in the other ("Sometimes," said Frank

* Lindsey Drummond, 1944.

·[134]·

Churchill, "one conjectures right and sometimes one conjectures wrong").

So I conjecture Mrs. Brown surviving death complete with what St. Thomas Aquinas calls her "intellectual memory." This is a very different affair from her "sensitive memory," which was always a poor thing and liable to let her down, and at its best could never recall more than one thing at a time. Her intellectual memory is nothing less than her whole past life, actually present —without the sense of merely being remembered. It is something like that vision said to appear before the eyes of drowning men, a vision possibly due to the failing at the point of death of cerebral control, of the "one thing at a time" mechanism. It must be a strange and terrible experience for Mrs. Brown to find herself alive again in her own memory—the actual, complete recovery of every single thing she ever did or said or thought.

> Lo, the book exactly worded,
> Wherein all has been recorded—
> Thence shall judgment be awarded.

Moreover, she is not, so to speak, alone, but in the company of Mr. Brown, of her son Sam who went to Australia and is still living, of the baby who did not survive its birth three days and was never baptized—to say nothing of that horrible woman next door and the quarrel she had with her and the things she said. They are all there; and there too is the sad episode of the half sovereign she covered with her thumb when its owner had left it lying on the counter . . . and a whole lot more . . . in fact, "every idle word" . . . and also, thank God, that lovely evening in spring when she walked home with Beatrice through the Easter lanes after her confirmation, and the blackbird's song fell like rain from a tree in Pondtail Shaw and the primroses were like yellow stars in the long grass by the ditches . . . and that time when she let Mrs. Claphouse go three weeks without paying her rent, because her husband was in hospital, and that time when she gave up her holiday to look after Mrs. Hodge who was having her third, and that time when she deliberately did *not* tell Miss Cooke what she thought of her. . . .

In that gigantic spectacle of recovery it is inevitable that certain very humble actors should play their humble parts. Not only is her husband there, but her dog Bonzo and her cat Nibs. This conjecture of mine gives them both a sort of immortality. They both survive, not in themselves but as part of Mrs. Brown's survival; she meets them both after death—together (if one is logical) with every fly she has ever swatted, every wasp that has ever stung her, and every one of those deplorable insects that came out of the wall at No. 7.

But to survive in someone else's memory is not immortality; especially if, as I conjecture, such survival is only temporary. Mr. Brown and Mrs. Claphouse and Mrs. Hodge and Miss Cooke and the woman next door survive death, not as parts of Mrs. Brown but in their own right—they all have their own personal, independent survivals apart from their place in hers, just as she survives apart from her place in theirs. But do Bonzo and Nibs survive independently? I doubt it.

I see that I have used the word "temporary," which shows how difficult it is to avoid the language of time when dealing with a situation in which time, at least as measured by the clock, has ceased to exist. But the end of clock time does not necessarily mean the end of duration. I do not expect Mrs. Brown to attain immediately after death—if she ever does—to that simultaneousness which is one of the divine attributes and will probably never be experienced, at least in its totality, by man. There is an extension, a movement of experience, in the course of which Bonzo and Nibs drop out— or rather are absorbed in certain key memories, which in their turn open like flowers in a transformation scene, revealing secret things which they have hidden. I will hopefully conjecture that Mrs. Brown's key memories are those of holiness and kindliness and that it is these not those of dishonesty, cruelty and carnality, which will shape her eternal life.

I see that life not as a straight line going on forever, but as a triangle rising from a line which is no longer than the length of her earthly years. She has no contemporaneous existence in some other world with events that have happened since her death in this one. The motion of her life is no longer parallel, but "away"—"upward" . . . at the very first she may have had some links with earth, even with time in a limited sense. But as the experiences of her past life, recovered in their totality at death, gradually lose their outwardness, their solid earthly shapes, and become more and more what they were in their essences, she enters a different world—as unlike this as a cake is unlike itself before it was baked.

Forgive the homely simile, but we are still (though I may seem to have forgotten it) in the kitchen, so perhaps I may be forgiven the conjecture that eternity bears the same relation to time as the cake I take out of the oven bears to its separate raw ingredients—to the eggs, the flour, the milk, the sugar, the fat, the flavoring, that were once spread out upon the kitchen table. They are all still there—nothing has been taken away, but everything is changed.

And here I think conjecture must stop. Already, perhaps, it has gone too far. But I may have been able to show why I cannot believe that Bonzo and Nibs survive in the same eternal sense as Mrs. Brown and why I could not, though I longed to do so, believe in the eternal survival of my cat.

He was at an end, except in a few small earthly memories, symbolized by the rosemary bush we planted on his grave. He lay among the poplars at the edge of his estate, beside the path he used to walk on every morning, going round the garden, looking at everything, like a fine old squire making his daily tour of inspection. I had done for him all I could and I could do no more for myself.

But comfort came in rather an unexpected way. For days I had felt the loss of my cat with a pain I knew was exaggerated, but which I could not assuage with mental nostrums. Then one evening, listening to the

radio, I heard a performance of Dr. Vaughan Williams'
setting of four poems by Skelton. This lovely work in-
cludes "Jane Scroop's Lament for Philip Sparrow"—the
lay of the little Tudor girl whose pet sparrow was dead,
who mourned him so bitterly that the kind nuns of
Carrow staged a requiem for him to comfort her. They
staged a requiem for Philip Sparrow, and it became the
requiem of my Johnny. "Oremus," they sang, tenderly,
sadly and yet with a smile, "Dominus vobiscum"—and
Philip Sparrow slept secure in the love and knowledge
of One without whom no sparrow falls to the ground,
no cat bows his head upon his paws to die. . . . Oh, kind
nuns of Carrow—and John Skelton and Dr. Vaughan
Williams and the B.B.C. Midland Orchestra—you gave
me my Johnny's requiem, and purged the ignorance
and foolishness out of me with a beauty which was also
wisdom. In other more prosaic words the music gave
me an emotional release which brought my abnormal
misery to an end, and enabled me not only to think
calmly and happily about my cat, but to give myself
calmly and happily to the business of acquiring another.

3.

WHEN IT CAME TO THE POINT, I ACQUIRED TWO;
for I could not make up my mind whether to
call up the echo of old times with a Persian or ring in
new ones with a Siamese. I had decided that I would not
have another long-haired blue, as the coat is a problem
always difficult and finally deadly, but I had been ad-
vised to try the short-haired Russian breed. In the end
a basket arrived containing a small blue plush bear,
which emitted a very unbearlike hissing sound. The bear-
like growls came from something more like a monkey,
a patchwork of brown and white, with blue eyes that
glowed furiously red at the sight of the little bear. For
the first evening all was growls and hisses; then order
was established, but never, I think, friendship.

I called those two Darcy and Bingley, but they grew up sorrily misnamed. Darcy, though descended from the Temple cats of Siam, was far from proud or aristocratic. Cats seldom are, except perhaps the long-haired blues. They have a reputation for aristocracy and elegance, but as a cat-loving friend observed to me, "cats are essentially middle-class." Darcy was middle-class to the backbone. Every morning saw him trotting off into the woods to earn his living, every evening saw him trotting home—you could almost see his attaché case and bowler hat.

He normally refused to eat our food until repeated visits to his place of business had shown him that nothing was to be had elsewhere. He was soon known to travel miles in search of a kill, and sometimes would come home with the bones of a hastily devoured rabbit sticking through his ribs, looking for all the world as if he had swallowed a bag of knitting. He must have had the gastric juices of an ostrich, for his figure would be normal after about an hour's siesta.

He did not sleep the light, aware sleep of a cat, but the heavy sleep of a dog. Indeed he had many doglike characteristics. His favorite game was a dog's game of retrieving a rabbit's foot, which I was required to throw tirelessly across the hall. It was not till he was grown-up that the feline element asserted itself and urged him to take the rabbit's foot to his den under a chair, instead of bringing it back to me.

Unlike any cat I have ever known he loved going out in the car. He would sit on a ledge under the rear window and gaze out at the road behind him, to the intrigue of following traffic. On foot he would follow us over the fields, a truly beautiful object leaping from tussock to tussock like a wild cat. At night he was capable of sleeping peacefully beside my bed, without demanding—after the usual cat manner—to be let out at unconscionable hours.

And yet, mercifully, with all these companionable ways, he was no talker—the conversation of a Siamese being one of those good things of which one can and generally does, have too much. (Incidentally, I regard it as a similar phenomenon to a dog's barking—if over-indulged in, a sign of nerves or irritation or some form of mismanagement.) Darcy never talked unless he had something to say, and then he said it briefly and not too loudly—the ideal conversationalist; but he also had the finest flow of bad language I had ever heard come from a cat. Most of it was lavished on the infant Tuesday, then starting his career as a garden cat, and seldom did he repeat himself in the course of an afternoon.

Bingley was a totally different personality, and per-haps a little more like his name, for he certainly played second-fiddle in the duet. I think he would have been a more attractive cat if we had had him alone, for all the time he was suffering from and reacting to comparisons. Darcy's doglike characteristics made him inevitably more popular, and poor Bingley had to fall back on buffoon-ery. He is the only cat I have even seen work to get a laugh. He grew to a terrific length of limb, and he soon realized the entertainment value of hanging himself through the banisters over the hall and waving his arms and torso in a semicircular motion for the beguilement of spectators. He would repeat the performance when required, and had a variation in which he emerged and waved from a half-shut drawer. He seemed delighted with the notice these feats attracted, but it is a sad day for a cat when he has to descend to low comedy for his effects.

I fear that he had few other qualities to recommend him. He seemed almost without affection, and would never appreciate the human lap as a resting place. He was also abnormally timid. Though he had never had a word of unkindness he persisted in treating us all as if our chief aim were his destruction. Especially was he appalled by our efforts to remove from his ears the rabbit lice that would inevitably cling to them after a visit to the warrens. He had the sensitive blue skin of his breed, and his ears were soon in a terrible condition

—unlike Darcy's, which seemed quite unaffected by a similar plague.

John Henry had also suffered terribly from these ticks, but he had always allowed us to remove them, whereas Bingley squealed with terror if anyone attempted to do so. In the end it became a veterinary job, with fresh cause for panic. We tried everything to prevent him from scratching his ears—a collar and then a bonnet, the patient work of hours demolished in seconds. The only effective cure was ten days' incarceration in the bathroom, as painful to us as to him; but that was brought to nothing within an hour of his release. He was, I am afraid, a senseless cat. There seemed nothing for him but euthanasia. The vet, however, had a better idea. All that was wrong with Bingley, he said, was living in the country. Put him in a town, where he could not visit rabbit warrens or catch rabbits and he would probably manage very well. It would be easy enough to find him a home; in fact he knew of a lady. . . .

So Bingley went off, with few regrets on our side and apparently none on his, to a neighboring seaside town, where he lived through over a thousand air raids before he had to be put to sleep because he would *not* stop scratching his ears.

Darcy was left as our only house cat, and at two years old had almost succeeded in filling the place left by the beloved Johnny. He was quite a different sort of cat, humbler, more hardworking; he gave himself no airs, and apparently indulged in no fancies. But he was faithful, affectionate, and beautiful—even though he had been bred with such old-fashioned Siamese points as a squint and a crooked tail.

Cats are notoriously beyond good and evil, indifferent to common rules of morality; yet it seems as if in revenge an aggressively moral destiny shapes their ends —certainly it shaped the ends of my three. John Henry died of the fur coat of which he was so outrageously vain, Bingley died because he was a fool who would not trust human beings or stop scratching his ears; and now my dear little Darcy was to die because he was a poacher.

One evening he never came home from his daily expedition to the woods. I looked for him everywhere, I called him everywhere; I searched every field, every thicket, every clump of thistles. The farm men visited every trap or where traps were rumored to be. I had a notice printed and displayed, but with no result beyond the printer's comment—"My! you must have been fond of that cat."

Then Somebody told my husband that Somebody who did not want his name mentioned, had told him that Somebody Else who still less wanted his name mentioned, had seen Something Strange in his field, and because he didn't know what it was he had shot it. It was a Siamese cat, and he had buried it. I was to be assured that he had buried it—that being apparently regarded as my chief concern. I had offered a substantial reward, but in this case anonymity was preferred to gain, and none of the Somebodies materialized into a more profitable existence. I believe, however, the story to be true. I believed it then, and it assuaged at least the terrors of imagination which in this case had been added to the woes of bereavement—picturing my Darcy as starving to death in a trap, lost among strangers (he had a habit of climbing into unknown cars) or even—believe it or not—stolen by gypsies and made to perform at fairs.

But the woes of bereavement remained, and this time I told myself that something drastic must be done. Twice in two years I had lived through a misery totally out of proportion to its cause, wasting the substance of grief on what should have asked for no more of me than its shadow. In the past I had known sorrows adequately grounded and the future was already dark with clouds of a whole world's wretchedness. I must not live on in this emotional jeopardy.

So I decided—not to give up keeping cats (which would not have worked at all, since cats would then have become both a hunger and a legend), but to keep the sort of cat I did not like, some low-bred Moggie who would never snare my heart with his beauty and intelligence. My old home had given me many disappointing experiences of tabby cats, who had all appeared unfriendly and without personality—partly, no doubt, because my mother filled their small capacities for love and friendship and partly because the cat is one of the few animals whose personal character seems to be improved by breeding, the process apparently making for intelligence rather than nerves as in the case of horses and dogs.

So I asked the vet (who combines the numerous and onerous duties of a country vet with being a sort of animal registry office), to find me a common tabby cat, and in due course out of a basket emerged, grinning, writhing, squirming, purring, scrabbling, waving, mepping, mewing Nikolous Ridikulous, the Cat to End All Cats. Even with my low expectations I was at first appalled—"It's dreadful—it's hideous—it hasn't even got green eyes—and it's wearing torn white gloves." I would have rejected him if my husband had not thought him rather pleasant (an opinion he has since revised) and if I had not been touched by the poor creature's evident desire to please and efforts to behave himself—carried to a desperate point of continence among lawns and flower beds, because he had, unknown to us, been trained only to use an ashpan.

He was called Nikolous by the parlormaid, because he came at Christmastime. The Ridikulous followed automatically—"Oh, Nikolous, don't be so Ridikulous— get away, you Ridikulous thing." The spelling, by the way, is the only part of the name I owe to Mr. Jacques Brown, for unlike John Henry this cat was not named after a radio star, and if Mr. Brown protests that Nikolous Ridikulous was one of his most famous parts, I can only say that I thought of the name before I heard him play it.

Nikolous has lived up to all my hopes of him. He has

·[143]·

been with us five years without producing in his mistress any more pathological symptom than irritation. We are quite pleased to see each other when we meet, and since becoming the cook I have taken considerable trouble to feed him and Tuesday in a manner for which (considering that it often involves my own rations) they ought to be sincerely grateful. But I have not given him my heart to tear—I never worry when he does not come home after a night out, and I can be extremely firm with him when, in true Rum-Tum Tugger fashion, he leaps into the middle of a fish soufflé.

My husband, by the way, says I am as bad as ever—the only difference being (as with many alleged cures) that I do not know it.

4.

I HAVE NEVER KEPT A DOG SINCE WE CAME TO LIVE IN the country. Not only were we discouraged by our experiment with the dachshund—for he was a neurotic little beast, prone to attacks of canine hysteria, and finally died of an abscess on the brain—but I am convinced in opposition to popular opinion that the country is no place for dogs; that is to say pet dogs. Gun dogs, sheep dogs, watchdogs, all these have their position in rural economy, but a dog which just hangs about the house and demands to be taken for "walkies" is nothing but a parasite, and a parasite moreover who often comes to a bad end among traps and guns.

I am not so perverted as to dislike dogs, and certainly they are not excluded from my affections by my love of cats, for cats are the very good friends of dogs they know, and indeed prefer them as housemates to other cats. But I cannot help echoing in my heart the sentiment I once heard expressed by a Belgian lady when she was asked why she did not keep a dog—"*Ils m'ennuient et ils demandent trop de soins.*" A dog bores me with two characteristics of which I am, I fear, intolerant—sentiment and flattery. He is also unable either to feed himself or to keep himself clean without my help. In plain language he is helpless and a humbug. There is no good talking to me about his companionship if he bores me, or of his devotion, if I believe at least fifty per cent of it to be either feigned or self-interested.

In saying this I do not think I am judging him unfairly, and I believe that what I dislike in him is the essence of his attraction for many people. Many people like their friends to be inferior, not superior, to themselves, and would probably deny that their dog's adoration, carried to the point of imitating their vices, has anything in it of insincerity. Many people, too, dislike an animal whose main idea in life is to look after himself—they call cats selfish and unfeeling, and because they do not as a rule take much notice of human beings they regard them as stupid.

Of course it is ridiculous to judge animals by moral and mental standards with which they have no concern. The plain facts are that the dog is a herd animal, with most of his natural instincts centered on the herd or the person who in civilization has taken the place of the herd; while the cat is a lone animal, with his natural instincts centered on the lone self and its habitation. The dog is helpless, because he is not designed to fend for himself apart from the herd or the herd representative—he is loving, because all his affections and loyalties are directed outside himself. The cat, on the other hand, must be self-regarding and self-supporting, or he would perish. These are the facts, and the rest is merely a matter of preference. Each animal follows perfectly the only moral code he knows—the code of natural law.

I own that a dog is more like ourselves and therefore it is easier for us to appreciate and understand him, whereas a certain effort of imagination is required to put ourselves in a cat's place. Cat lovers are either imaginative people or else people who, for some reason, are rather like cats—people who like to be alone, who do not wear their hearts on their sleeves, who find it easier to become attached to places than to other people, who when they meet anything they dislike do not bark at it but walk away and sit down with their backs turned.

No animal has perhaps been more damaged by his association with civilization than the cat—his association with mankind has brought him no blessing. The dog, on the other hand, has profited by the diversion of his loyalty from a gang of equals to a small number of superiors. He has moved very much higher than his wild origins, whether as found in the wolf or in the wretched pariah dog of the East. He has adapted himself to human life, which has enlarged and deepened his faculties. I do not think that we human beings have any serious grounds for self-reproach on his account. Even if he copies our vices as well as our virtues, he is still very much improved by our company.

The cat, however, has an altogether different story. As a wild beast he is royal—the lion, in fact. Even as a wild cat, though savage as hell, he is glorious with a glory that no fireside puss can know save perhaps in dreams. We have worshiped him as god, but we have none the less degraded him. We have taken from him his integrity and then despised him for lacking that which we have robbed him of.

The wild cat throughout his days is the faithful husband of one wife. The pair have one litter a year, or at the most two. They rear the young together in their den in the woods or among the rocks, hunting for them together, watching over them together after the honest manner of foxes and badgers till maturity disbands them to the freedom of their own mating.

By some means we tempted cats out of this Eden. Did they fall through luxury or pride?—were they enticed by cushions and cream or by divine honors to be paid them? Who shall say? But man at least should feel for them the sympathy of a common fate—lured out of paradise to "be as gods" and then finding themselves in the back yard among the rubbish and the old tin cans. Certainly in sorrow they now bring forth their seed, for man has taken upon himself to drown their females and castrate their males. The race can no longer be maintained by monogamy. So the rare female becomes what has been rightly called a kitten factory, while the rare, ragged, hunting, hunted male, procreates his kind in polygamy and incest.

This is the dark side of the picture. The brighter, more estimable side, is the determination of cats to carry on their breed in spite of all the obstacles which men have put in their way. Their exaggerated fertility is their counteroffensive to our attack on their procreation. In the male it is not inspiring, but in the female it has led to what must surely be the most beautiful example of intelligent and devoted mother love in the animal kingdom. To maintain the race the kittens must not only be born, but be preserved and trained to survive. (Query, is it a maneuver on the part of nature that the sex of young kittens should be so difficult to distinguish that a number of females are inadvertently spared?) The mother cat not only feeds her young, not only protects them with her own life if necessary, but trains and educates them. She is the only animal I know who seems to exercise discipline in the home. Young kittens are controlled, smacked, ordered about, washed, combed, taught to perform their functions decently and politely. They are initiated into the mysteries of hunting by all sorts of games of tracking and pouncing, they are given object lessons in the shape of a rabbit's foot or a dead mouse, which the mother will bring into the den (your hat box) when they are far too young to do more than play with it.

Most cats have an ideally happy childhood (if they do not it is generally human mismanagement and not their mother's which is to blame), and as a result the cat is the only animal I know which seems to have a definite infancy fixation. Nearly all cats grow up with "a creeping lust for milk," the precious food of their childhood, never to be forgotten among later luxuries of fish and meat. They also preserve the movement that secured it for them, when their little arms pounded the warm soft-

·[147]·

ness from which it came. A cat trampling a rug is not, I am convinced, "trampling down the jungle grass," as the most common theory explains it. The softness reminds him of his mother's flank and those exquisite moments of warmth and nourishment, which his present action unconsciously seeks to restore. Never have I seen such an ecstasy of contentment as recently I saw on a little black face the size of half a crown . . . all his life that cat will seek to recapture the first month of his existence. The cushioned chair, the glowing fire, the saucer of fresh milk, the stroking hand will all be to him so many nostalgic fragments of the past which he relives in them.

In human beings a childhood fixation is unhealthy, a sign of neurosis; and it is probably the same in cats—one of the results of our interference with their private lives. On the whole I should say that we have a bad racial conscience toward them—my evidence being the fact that so many of us regard them abnormally. On one side we have the phobiac whose skin creeps with horror to tell him that an invisible cat is in the room; on the other we have the fanatic who would rather give his heart to be sneered at by an alley cat than effortlessly receive the devotion of the most faithful hound in all poetry and romance. Between are few gradations of normal affection and understanding. The majority of the human race ignores cats and avoids close relations with them—probably another sign of guilt. Oh, Puss, what have we done to you?—and what have you done to us?

5.

BUT THOUGH CATS ARE THE ONLY ANIMALS IN MY kitchen—there are a number of others outside it. Or it may be incorrect to say these are not in the kitchen, since they, most of them, enter it sooner or later. But they enter it much as human beings finally enter the churchyard, unaware of their last resting place. It is their cemetery, or rather, I should say their crematorium; for though the fire does not consume them it transmutes them into something other than their old selves. They become the food of those who fed them, and are absorbed into a Larger Consciousness. In other words I keep an outdoor larder of hens, ducks and rabbits.

The hens are the remnant of what in prewar days used to be a prosperous chicken farm. Once a week a huge van from a huge packing station called to take away cratefuls of our eggs, while one of the leading poulterers in the nearest seaside town sold our table birds. When the war began we thought, in our innocence, that our going concern would go very much further. We thought, in our ignorance, that owing to the reduction of imports, those foreign eggs which had so continuously spoiled our market in times of peace would be eliminated; we did not imagine that our own would share in that elimination. So we increased our stock and appliances, bought a number of pedigreed cockerels and felt proud of ourselves as an important unit of the national food supply.

The first hint to the contrary came from the War Agricultural Committee, a member of which (the same who had to wait an hour for his tea because I did not know how to boil the electric kettle) warned us that the government did not consider eggs an essential article of diet. They were prepared, he said, to keep the country alive and reasonably healthy on cereals, milk and—the nursery thank heaven for that gleam in Nanny's eye— beer. Mercifully we did not come to this, but the reader does not require to be told that eggs have had a very peculiar history since Dunkirk.

They now have ceased to be simply eggs, but are divided into shell eggs and dried eggs, while the former are again subdivided into those coming from the shop and those coming from the hen. The keeping of poultry is one of the few matters in which the government has given preference to the small man, and the country is full of Domestic Poultry Keepers, keeping hens either for

·[149]·

family use or for a few customers, while the big farms have been driven out of existence, except for certain accredited breeding stations.

It is, of course, a question of shipping space, which cannot be spared for the importation of poultry food. The Domestic Poultry Keeper can keep his flock in very good condition on household scraps mixed with balancer meal, but it would take a camp to provide enough swill for a full-sized poultry farm. Our farm came to an end through the sudden withdrawal of rations—officially on account of a technical flaw in the lease of certain fields, through which our supplies became diverted to a tenant who did not keep poultry, but also possibly (according to local rumor, backed by subsequent events) because the Ministry had orders to drive out of business every poultry farmer who did not depend on his farm for a living. There is no question but that the distinction was fair and the situation demanded it and we had neither the right nor the wish to complain. All I could have asked was that the Ministry in its dealings with us had not treated us so unrelentingly as criminals. By the time it was all over I felt as if, far from helping my country's food supply I had prolonged the war for another ten years.

I am now reduced to the ranks, in other words, I have become a Domestic Poultry Keeper, with eight registered customers, who, I was warned, would be my inveterate enemies by the end of the first month. With none of them in the course of three years have I ever had the slightest altercation.

Speaking selfishly, the egg situation is very much better than when we had the farm. For in those days we gave to the packing station everything we could possibly spare, drastically curtailing our own use, whereas now we find that a dozen hens and three ducks allow ten people to use eggs with almost peacetime lavishness for the greater part of the year. My hens have enabled me to specialize in a delicious spongecake, which in the old days I should have regarded as treasonable, but

·[150]·

which I can now call an economy, since it uses no butter or margarine.

Another advantage is that I have entered into much more satisfactory personal relations with my flock. When we had several hundred hens it was impossible to know them all personally, and as a result I formed an entirely erroneous idea of a hen's character. In a novel of mine, *Ember Lane*, a poultry farmer's wife speaks thus of her hens. I quote with shame.

> One of the least pleasant contrasts between poultry and general farming was the difficulty of feeling any sort of personal affection for the stock . . . these hens seemed less individualized than sheep, less sensitive than fish, and her feeling for them was entirely practical and financial, such as she imagined a grocer might feel for his lumps of lard and tins of tea. When she shut the houses for the night their heads, as she saw them above the shutter, seemed to suggest no more of life and laughter than a row of umbrella handles and walking sticks. As far as any affectionate emotion was concerned she would not have minded finding them all dead next morning.

Those were my sentiments as a full-scale poultry farmer, but—except for the fact that hens' heads are indeed remarkably like the handles of umbrellas and walking sticks—none of it is true now. All my hens have personalities, and so far from indifferent am I to their decease that I am now uneconomically keeping alive at least six elderly ladies who should long ago have been simmered. They are the only survivors of the original poultry farm, and their old age is hallowed by golden memories of glories past. With them still runs the cock whom we had sent down from Yorkshire, traveling so proudly in his cock-basket, and emerging so gaily after his twelve-hour journey to immediate nuptials with many delighted brides.

I have read in every bulletin of advice to Domestic

Poultry Keepers that it is quite unnecessary to run a cock with hens; they perform their main function equally well as spinsters. This is true, of course, as far as it goes. The presence or absence of the cock does not affect the laying, except in so far as his presence makes for that contentment and bonhomie which are essential to egg production. But he is invaluable to the weary henwife by virtue of his excellent habit of taking the hens to bed at a godly hour. Not in vain is he called a rooster. If he had charge of all my hens, I should be able to go to bed at least half an hour earlier than I do in double summertime.

He is also an abater of internecine strife. I started my domestic flock with individuals culled from a dozen runs, and not one cross word was ever uttered so far as I am aware. But when I tried in my own strength to amalgamate three pullets who had just come into lay with three slightly older birds whom they had known for months as next-door neighbors, the result was a battle of which I tired before the combatants. Hens are, I fear, ill-natured and unkind to one another. They have a selfish, each-woman-for-herself pattern of behavior, which needs a cock's control. I should have liked to give him the lot, but fear that at his advanced age they would be too many for him.

But he shall not follow his hens into the pot. He shall live to enjoy the delightful and unusual experience of exchanging six elderly wives for six beautiful young ones. Candidly, I cannot bear to part with him. He is my very good friend. Every day he waits for me at the entrance to the chicken run; nothing in that, of course—they all do it. But his interest is not centered on his feeding trough but in the little basket that I carry. In it there is always a special titbit for him. Not long ago it would be a few oats, salvaged from rats or got by gleaning, but now I am afraid that it is cake. He loves cake more than anything on earth, and I hope I may be forgiven for giving him all the hard outside pieces and stale heels that come my way. He stretches his neck to a swan's length, so that he can look into my basket and make sure that I have brought him what he wants; and never would anyone believe that a gnarled red umbrella handle decorated with two round red beads could express so much emotion—such desire, such anticipation, such entreaty. . . .

But his gratification must wait till he has escorted his hens to their meal and attended to their wants. Then, when he sees me on my way back to the storehouse from the rabbit hutches, he officially breaks up the party at the trough and brings them with him to enjoy a sort of dessert. His hens are, I fear, a set of greedy, unmannerly old baggages, who will snatch the food out of my hand before he can reach it, or indeed out of his mouth. There is one—a Rhode Island-Sussex cross who has the peculiarity of having, unlike most hens, a full face instead of only a profile—whom I have seen actually put her beak into his and pull the cake out of his throat. Yet he never defends himself and if I attempt to drive her off he is indignant, flaps his wings and walks away, rebuking me.

It is very difficult not to transgress some unknown rule of animal etiquette. Those who speak of the farmyard in terms of libertinism and license have really no idea what they are talking about. A farmyard is much more like one of our more conservative public schools, ridden with rules, customs, shibboleths, survivals. One is perpetually proclaiming oneself a bounder. As for cats— I know from experience that catiquette is a science which even the most devoted student never fully masters.

My old cock is a fiend for ceremony. When he brings his hens to dessert he always first leads them solemnly in a procession round the storehouse where I am busy with the mash pails. If I do not come out when he has been round once, he leads them round again, and I imagine would go on round and round indefinitely till I appeared. As he goes he makes a queer gobbling sound, no doubt his magic word, his abracadabra or Open Sesame though in his case it sounds more like the name of a Mexican volcano—Pocolocolotl, Pocoloco-lotl. . . . He is working a magic rite, producing food for his family, going round the mulberry bush after the manner of primitive man.

I have not the heart to upset his calculations by coming out empty-handed. The magic always works. Yet at the door always stand the skeptic—the one hen who does not go round, but stands watching me with a humorous, doubting eye, and gets her portion all the same. Bunkum, she says—Mumbo Jumbo. . . . But he still says Pocolocolotl, Pocolocolotl.

When I first observed his behavior I thought I saw in it the elements of reason, an attempted research on his part into the laws of cause and effect. But as I watched I came to doubt if there was any reason or indeed any thought in it at all. The rite seems rather to be based on an automatic association of ideas. At one time I must have come out of the lodge just after he had walked round it and given him something he fancied. As a result when next he wanted a titbit his desire revived the memory of that earlier occasion and an association of desire and memory compelled a repetition of the behavior, which he probably saw as a complete whole—i. e., the trot round the lodge not so much leading to the enjoyment of the cake as an actual part of its enjoyment.

This of course is only another of those conjectures in which I find recreation while I stir the soup or beat the eggs and sugar for the spongecake ("not less than twenty minutes" says the inexorable Mrs. Beeton). It is connected with another surmise—that superstition is nothing but a throwback to early misinterpretations of the law of cause and effect. In the state of knowledge available to them, it was not unreasonable for prehistoric men to believe in the influence of certain natural objects, such as stones or trees, or of certain mysterious new conceptions such as numbers and colors. There would be nothing in their science to show that two events immediately succeeding each other were not necessarily connected—as, for instance, the death of a relative and the gift of a precious stone or the failure of a hunting party to return and. its last-minute increase from twelve to thirteen.

In believing these things they were not following the same pattern of behavior as my old cock. Their associations at least were rationalized, even supposing that they were not based on observation and reflection. They were not betraying their own intelligence as are their modern descendants when they accept their conclusions. These conclusions have had to be revised in the light of greater knowledge—like the conclusions of Ptolemy as to the place of the earth in the solar system. But as it would be the sheerest provincialism to sneer at Ptolemy for his deductions from the facts in his possession, so I think it would be a display of ignorance to sneer at those primitive philosophers who founded our superstitions in the science of their day.

We, no doubt, are founding fresh superstitions for generations to come, out of the ignorances and misconceptions that bound our knowledge. In fact I should not be surprised if we should leave more superstition behind us than any primitive community. For though our knowledge is far greater I do not think our mental processes are so free; they seem to me more automatic and constricted—more like my rooster's. It is my melancholy surmise that as education becomes more widespread we find more and more automatons, more and more laziness in following well-worn cerebral tracks. If primitive man had used no more of his brain than we do he would have perished from the face of the earth.

As knowledge increases, our ideas contrive to get bunched into bigger and bigger associations, so that we can think quite a lot without using other than semi-automatic possessions. Everything in our civilization—from the press with its "stunts" and the advertisements with their "slogans" to the propaganda of total war with its catchwords and general tendency to mulctify the intellect—conspires to enlarge and solidify these amalgamations. The contrast between the civilized and the primitive mind becomes the contrast between a neatly paved and placarded town, through which we may walk with scarcely a thought to our direction, and a wild piece of country which demands all our faculties if we are to find our way across it.

Civilization enlarges our towns metaphorically as well as literally. Our mental as well as our domestic furniture is more and more mass-produced, our thoughts as well as our clothes are increasingly "ready-to-wear." And yet not long ago I read in one of our more thoughtful weeklies that a formidable objection to the idea of human survival was the difficulty of imagining prehistoric man in heaven. The difficulties my imagination has to contend with are of an exactly opposite nature. They are the same as those expressed by my late friend and literary godfather, W. L. George, who, when for some reason we became involved in a theological discussion in a Piccadilly teashop and I asked him why he did not believe in the immortality of the soul, pointed across the road and said briefly: "Fortnum and Mason." I leave the reader with this thought, which, though ready-made, is not ready-to-wear, and return to my living larder.

6.

BETWEEN HENS AND DUCKS A VAST PSYCHOLOGICAL GULF is fixed. I find that hens, though inclined to unnecessary fluster, are in the main regular and dependable in their habits. They are model mothers and at the same time without the smallest pin point of affection for their fellow hens. As to their married life, the cock is always master—I have never yet seen him henpecked. On the other hand, hens seem to have none of the pleasures of courtship. A cockerel treads without noticeable preliminaries and certainly no noticeable enjoyment on the part of his spouse.

Ducks, on the contrary, are as full of temperament as

·[156]·

any prima donna in fiction. As a handbook on duck-keeping understates it: "ducks are very easily upset." I have had to let myself be drenched with pouring rain because my ducks had taken a dislike to my waterproof and would not let me come near them while I was wearing it (Did they think it a usurpation of their own immunity to showers?). In further contrast, they are shocking mothers, and their neglect and cynical indifference to their progeny begins with the egg, which they will lay anywhere—in the middle of the road or even in the middle of the pond. This is not an abnormality due to their civilization, because a wild duck is just as casual. It is true that she takes more trouble to make a clutch, but I know at least one case in which its successful hatching was due to the care and attention of a farmer's boy. He did not actually sit on the eggs, but it was about the only part of the work he did not do for her.

As against this, ducks are quite beautifully devoted to one another. Once I had a drake too many, and in order to stop the incessant fights over an inadequate supply of ducks I had him killed for the pot. Never were such lamentations, such searchings for the lost one with such pathetic calls and cries. His rival joined in the universal woe, and his widow (for he was in possession of only one wife at the time of decease) threatened to be inconsolable. I made a vow that next time I killed I would kill the lot.

Incidentally, though a drake has normally only a couple of wives, he is far more henpecked than a rooster who has twenty. My surviving drake was shamelessly bundled about by his females, including Widow Waddleby, who in course of time became the leader and dictator of the party. Mr. Walt Disney can never have kept ducks, or he would know that the stridencies of his Donald never opened a male beak (unless American ducks are a species apart). My drake could make only a low muttering sound, which one heard as a sort of obbligato accompaniment to the ear-splitting racket of his spouses. They certainly had a vast power of larynx and of lung. When feeding time approached (and their clock was remarkably accurate) the sentinel duck then on duty would greet in tones similar to those which interrupted Mickey's band concert any sound which at any time had ever preceded the arrival of food. Shy guests would be embarrassed by the clamor which broke forth at the closing of a door or the pulling of a plug; while anyone who arrived by car would find a reception committee of three ducks and a drake bowing on the doorstep.

Bowing is a notable part of a duck's courtship rites but seems transferable to feeding. In spring their meals would be made to a low, soft, gabbling accompaniment —not unlike a psalm recited "without tone." But these were preliminaries only. The meal itself was an orgy of gobbling and spewing from which I have returned with mash in my hair.

These ducks were survivors of the poultry farm, kept for their eggs after their brothers and sisters had helped solve our food problem on more total lines. We left them free to feed themselves, giving them a meal only at night, so that we could shut them up and collect their eggs the next morning. They must have roamed miles by day, traveling in a little muttering, beak-to-tail procession, from pond to pond, but always coming home in the evening, to summon us with loud whoops from the pond, or if that failed, to waddle to the house and quack under the front door.

Waddleby was the only one who had a name; her method of walking had been remarkable from the first. Even for a duck it was outstanding. She had a way of throwing out her legs at right angles to her body, which rocked her like a cradle. Curiously enough her advance was extremely rapid—one had almost to run to keep up with her, and she always led the procession, forging to the head of it if ever she started at the tail. At first we called her Mrs. Waddleby, then plain Waddleby; finally for some reason she became La Waddleby.

I loved her dearly with her prima donna temperament

and washerwoman ways, and it was a real grief to me when I realized that apart from her personal charms her existence was no longer justified. Ducks are not so de-natured as to lay all the year round, and after she had finished her second season's effort I was bullied and per-suaded into believing that it would not be profitable to feed her for nine months in anticipation of a greatly reduced output in the third year. My hand was finally forced by the kind gift of three young ducks, which made it impossible to keep the old ones, as rations could not be stretched to feed six.

So I gave the order for her execution—"her" includ-ing her three companions, for I was still determined to have no heartbroken survivors. I did not even keep the drake, though I was told that he would be useful with the new ducks. I do not believe it—I believe that he would have died of a broken heart after wringing mine to anguish. Drakes have not the facile, transferable affections of roosters.

I never felt a farmyard death more than I felt dear Waddleby's, especially as her successors have proved so unworthy that I am keeping them only till the green peas are ripe. I have said that she had the temperament of a prima donna; so have they, but it is the prima donna of a lunatic asylum—in which I feel we shall all join them if we keep them much longer. They have been with me now for six months, and yet they persist in treating me as their sub-greatest enemy, the greatest of all being poor kind old Fuggle, our farm hand, of whom they are so terrified that (the condition being in-fectious) he dare not collect their eggs if they are any-where near. He is deeply hurt—"I handled 'em—dat's what it is—I handled 'em, and *dey can't forgive me.*"

I am deeply hurt too, for though I have never handled them (heaven forbid!) they flee at my approach, even if I carry their mash bucket, and from a safe distance, with stretched necks and wide-open beaks, make hideous faces at me. I know that allowances must be made for ducks acquired full grown, but I think these have gone too far for any normal explanation of their hostility. "I reckon a wild duck flew in from de marsh and treeded deir mother," says old Fuggle, and he is probably right.

Waddleby made a glorious end—that is my great comfort. I do not refer to her behavior on the scaffold, of which I took care to have no knowledge, but of her almost apocalyptic passing into our systems in the form of roast duck.

Yes, *roast* duck. For though Waddleby was three years old, and had a mileage of probably three figures, she "cut up" as tender, succulent, and juicy as any duckling. This miracle was achieved by an old cook of mine, who came out from the seaside town to perform the ceremony. I pass on her recipe—or rather rite—for it is applicable to elderly hens as well as elderly ducks.

Rite for Cooking the Oldest Inhabitant of the Farmyard. 1. First hang the carcass for as long as you possibly can, according to the weather. Waddleby hung a week, already plucked and drawn, and her presence in the larder aroused no reminiscent sadness, for after having laid some hundred monster eggs (one was so big that it had to be served in the mouth of a jam jar) she looked more like a tunnel than a duck. 2. On the evening before the ceremony take an eggcupful of whisky and with a pastry brush paint it over the entire skin. This is essential—the magic does not work without whisky. 3. Repeat this two or three times on the day itself. I am presupposing that the meal is in the evening; if it is at midday, everything must be started earlier. The amount of whisky is enough for several anointings. 4. Put the carcass in a *covered* roasting tin into which you have poured water instead of fat, and cook in a brisk oven until all the water has evaporated, which should take about an hour. The reason for the whisky is now apparent, for you are steaming your bird; but the action of the alcohol on the skin will prevent this from getting soggy, after the manner of those aged fowls which appeared as *poulet rôti* in certain restaurants even before the war. 5. When all the water is gone, lower the heat, put dripping into the tin and baste frequently till the bird is cooked, which should take another two hours.

7.

I TURN RELUCTANTLY FROM THE COMPANIONABLE intelligence of the hen-run and the duckpond to the imbecility of the rabbit hutch: I knew nothing of rabbits before I started keeping them as a war measure, and I must confess that I was disappointed. They are so attractive in their looks and ways that it comes as a shock to discover that they are without either natural sagacity or natural affection. They are not wise enough to keep themselves or their offspring alive in the face of the smallest opposition on the part of nature, and their maternal behavior—generally the highest display of an animal's powers—seems to be as automatic as the wriggling of their noses.

A good mother will feed her young and keep them covered in a warm nest—uncovering them when the day is hot and tucking them up again as it grows cooler. But that these actions are practically reflex was shown me by a doe who for some reason got her rhythm wrong, covering up her youngsters in the noonday heat and uncovering them at night, with the result that they died of exposure. The average doe, moreover, seems not only helpless but indifferent to any fatality among her brood. I once saw an otherwise excellent mother calmly nibbling a lettuce leaf while one of her youngsters lay drowned in the drinking water at her side. One has only to picture a cat in a similar situation to realize what could be done in the way of practical and emotional reaction.

But rabbits might be nature's stepchildren, so meanly has she endowed them. She has given them no weapons, either of offense or of defense, and no cunning of mind to supply the deficiency. They are fleet, but no fleeter than some of their enemies and their camouflage —otherwise good—is spoiled by their white scuts.

They succumb easily to disease, and especially cruel seems their liability to be wiped out by their natural way of feeding. When the grass and other green meat is sodden with rain or dew the water collects in their guts and ultimately kills them. In a wet season dozens of rabbits can be found dead in the fields, swollen like the corpses of the drowned. This has given rise to the idea that in captivity they should never be given water. When a number of mine died one year I was told that this was the reason; but the removal of the water made no difference to the casualties, while the careful drying of their foodstuff (not till desiccated, but till "clung") brought them to an end almost at once. Rabbits do not drink much—in fact some of mine never drink at all; but I always keep them supplied with water, because I have seen others, especially does in kindle or with youngsters, sup up a whole dishful.

So ill-equipped is the rabbit race that it survives only by mass-production. Fertility is its one weapon against disease, gun, trap, snare, stoat, ferret, fox, and other forms of destruction. I must say that it has proved remarkably efficient; one shudders to think what the world would be like if rabbits had no enemies. In a single year a doe will rear at least three litters of seven or more youngsters each, and by the autumn each doe of the first, if not the first two, litters will have made her a grandmother. She will do the same next year and the next, and so will they, and so will those they have themselves produced, till the figures approach the measurements of the Milky Way.

When rabbits really become too many for the ground they are on, epidemics break out among them and the survivors migrate. This had happened here just before the war, and as a result there were no wild rabbits when we wanted them most for our larder. Their absence was of course a great blessing to the new plowlands, and therefore to us; but we missed them in our wartime kitchen.

Once or twice I tried the substitute of a gray squirrel, but gave it up for sheer lack of moral courage. The meat

I found excellent, better flavored than a rabbit's, and making a very tasty stew with onion and coarse oatmeal. There was not much on them except the two hind legs, but they made a nice little meal for two people, and we should probably still be enjoying them if I could have continued to face the disapproval of Joe Boorman, who shot them for us. Neither my husband nor I can do anything with a gun, so we had to rely on Joe, who is so smart with one that he can bring down even these most elusive pests. They are hideously destructive little beasts and he never failed to shoot one if he had the chance, but it obviously hurt him to see us eat it. By doing so we sank to the level of gypsies, and nothing short of siege conditions, in which men eat cats and rats, could really have excused us.

So I gave up asking for them and bought a couple of breeding rabbits. The rest was easy, for rabbits in captivity are excellently simple to keep. I am told that in Germany it is compulsory for country dwellers to keep them, and I marvel less at this than at the fact that so few keep them over here; for they are very little trouble to look after and cost nothing to feed. Unlike the hen, whose profitable support is the headache of more than one Ministry, they live almost entirely on garden and household surpluses. Verily they are the poor people's children, eating contentedly what others have thrown away—the outside leaves of cabbages and cauliflowers, carrots unfit for human food, leftover bits of toast or stale bread (epicurean delicacies these) and even tea-leaves. Their hutches are easy to keep clean and their feeding time can be limited to once a day, though twice is better. In return for this small amount of attention, two or three breeding does will feed a family all the year round. I calculate that my own small concern will provide a five or six pound carcass every fortnight for ourselves or our neighbors.

The objection is, of course, that rabbit meat wants such various cooking if one is not to weary of it. In my childhood it was always boiled with onion, and that is still, I fear, what rabbit means to most people. Not long ago at a well-known provincial hotel the only choice was between rabbit boiled and rabbit stewed. But rabbits can be roasted (with stuffing and bread sauce), fried (very young rabbits fried whole and served on toast are perfectly delicious), made into pies, cooked *à la marengo* with Spanish sauce and tomato, or with Béchamel sauce and mushrooms, or (if you are lucky) with cream and white wine. I have already described how they make a better chicken mousse than any chicken, and the same goes for chicken galantine. The liquor in which they are cooked is all but chicken soup, and can be made into jellied molds with a filling of diced rabbit meat and slices of hard-boiled egg.

Of course they have been very frequently cooked in such ways in peacetime; but as they were always chicken on the menu, the snobs have not been converted. Last time I ate rabbit in a London restaurant it was called game pie, and I must confess that it tasted remarkably like it.

Outside the menu, rabbits seldom achieve the dignity of names. They are both too numerous and too little individualized for such a distinction. Most of my rabbits have had only collective family names—such as the Rampagers or the Ravenoids or the Septarchy or the Poddies, according to the main mass characteristic of their litter. Only a few have been promoted to separate personalities.

Silversides was a huge and handsome buck, a mixture of Flemish Giant and Chinchilla Rex. He must have measured almost a yard from the ground to the tips of his ears, as he sat in his favorite attitude, on his haunches, with his gray forepaws hanging foolishly against his snow-white belly. In the twilight, when I went to shut the hen-houses, Silversides would rise up in his run like a ghost.

He was deeply interested in all that went on in the poultry field, where he and the other rabbits had their portable folds in summertime. A tall, inquiring figure he would watch the hens being fed, and he alone of all the rabbits seemed to take any pleasure in their company. Indeed, he would definitely try to attract their attention.

If a hen approached he would thump with his hind legs, and then bounce and skip till he had induced her to stand and watch him and indulge in a series of antics. His efforts at entertainment were not unappreciated, and I have known a whole group of hens to rush up when he began to thump, like children summoned by the drum to a Punch and Judy show. Only once have I seen his act despised. He started it, but the audience—a single hen—walked away with a bored expression before he was halfway through. Poor Silversides! To few even of the most unsuccessful of us can it have fallen to be given the bird by a hen.

Flora was another rabbit with a name and a personality. She was unusual in appearance, for though a purebred Flemish doe, her coat was a delicate fawn—a lovely shade, which being a sport of breeding and not a true characteristic she never, as we had hoped, passed on to her offspring. She was gay and debonair, wearing her ears like a hat, in a flighty, rakish way. She had more beauty than brains, and when her youngsters reached the runabout stage we had to take care that she did not starve, for she seemed quite unable to cope with their inroads on her provender or maintain her own end of the cabbage leaf. Nor had she any knowledge of the Facts of Life. Five minutes after the buck had visited her she would be busily making a nest for the youngsters which would not appear till thirty-one days later. She seemed to take a definite pleasure in having a family, and if we left her any time unmated, a nest would appear as a gentle hint. Her nests looked charming, with their central muff of beige fur, and she did not mind in the least if we handled her youngsters.

I was really fond of her and bitterly mourned her loss by enemy action just after she had brought nine beautiful babies into the world. The enemy this time did not come out of the sky but out of the wood—that Hitler of the farms still known in Sussex as Mus' Reynolds. One morning old Fuggle was at the door gibbering with rage and distress. Mus' Reynolds—or rather, I suspect, Mis' Reynolds, hunting for her cubs—had visited the poultry run during the night, and though mercifully he had not touched the hens, which were shut up in their houses, he had killed every one of my rabbits, except poor Flora's babies, which either he had missed or considered too small meat. From some of the runs he had torn the wire netting, others he had dragged away from the hutches, though one at least was too heavy for me to move singlehanded. He had eaten only one nameless rabbit and a part of darling Flora. The rest lay waiting for him to come again the next night. It was a heartbreaking affair, especially as we had to drown the nine surviving youngsters, having no means of feeding them.

The corpses, however, provided the whole neighborhood with rabbit pie. They had none of them been spoiled for human food, for Mus' Reynolds kills rabbits with a scissor-bite over the heart. My own share of the massacre was Silversides, in honor of whom I cast economy to the winds and used Mrs. Beeton's recipe for "rich short crust."

A few days later old Fuggle arrived with a sack over his handlebars. The sack contained a doe and nine youngsters, and the next day a doe and seven youngsters were similarly transported. I bought a pedigreed sable doe from a local fancier, and off we went again—this time keeping the whole lot indoors.

By the end of six months we had overflowed the lodge, and thought we might venture on two chicken arks outside it, the fronts of which we barricaded at night with sheets of corrugated iron. But Mus' Reynolds was not deterred even by this fortress. A few nights later he was back and had succeeded in pushing aside both pieces of iron, though they were held in place with spiles. He then started gnawing the doors open, but must have been interrupted, for he never actually broke in. Since then I have never kept a rabbit out of doors, and it is remarkable that their health in small indoor hutches is very much better than it was when I kept them in outdoor runs, when many of them perished through eating grass when it was wet with rain or dew.

These two experiences have entirely changed my

opinion of our local hunt, which before the war I had constantly abused for its inefficiency. I had always maintained that the only way to keep down foxes was by shooting and poisoning them, but certainly we have never been so plagued as since we have had to fall back on these methods. The foxes have been almost cynical in their defiance of us, appearing in broad daylight, so that I have had to give up that most excellent and profitable custom of putting out my fowls on the grattens, as the September stubble fields are called in these parts. The tragedy of my rabbits was followed by a spate of fox stories, as a fox looked at Mrs. Boorman through the hedge, or made Nellie jump when she went to hang out the clothes, or was heard by old Fuggle "going yip-yip, yip-yip, all de way up de lane."

We should, of course, have put strychnine into one of the rabbit corpses after the first visit; but I am always reluctant to adopt this plan, which endangers the innocent as well as the guilty. We organized a fox shoot, but it came back empty-handed, and though much later Joe Boorman shot a fox in Marlpit Wood, he did not kill it. A fox is an extremely difficult animal to shoot, as he travels long distances from home and at untoward hours. He also takes some killing, and there is, at the time, a dearth of the right sort of cartridges. But I have not ceased to live in hope of again seeing Joe as I once saw him many years ago (when, I fear, our hunt was still in action) standing at the door holding by the tail what in the dim light looked like the corpse of an Alsatian dog. I still hope for the triumph of wearing on my shoulders the orange pelt of the enemy of my little people.

8.

THE FOX IS NOT THE ONLY ENEMY THAT COMES OUT of the wood. From its ambushes also descend upon us wood pigeons, jays and magpies threatening and ravishing our kitchen garden. The wood is only about six yards from our back door, and as a result our garden birds are of quite a different sort from those in the village. This has its advantages as well as its drawbacks, for though I personally should like more thrushes and blackbirds, I can for the joy of the wood pigeon's note in June gladly relinquish them to the suburbs.

The cuckoo haunts us, and our eyes and ears have shown us that, contrary to the usual opinion, he sings as he flies. In May the nightingale serenades our moon, though for some reason he is no longer so close to the house as he used to be. There was a time when his song floated in at my bedroom window all night from a tree near the pond; and one night, I remember, he sang so clearly and constantly and the moon shone so brightly that the cuckoo woke and accompanied him for an hour. Moonlight, nightingale and cuckoo, scent of honeysuckle and scent of hay . . . all seemed to mingle and flow together. Seeing, hearing and smelling were no longer distinct but a single sensation. There are many such nights in the country.

Our present nightingale has chosen a more distant territory. Double summertime, moreover, interferes with our delight in him, as we are generally asleep before he tunes up with those scattered notes and trial warblings, which seldom used to be heard till after eleven and now do not come on the air till midnight is past. Only an occasional late night shows us that he is still there with his music.

I should like to know why he, or rather his descendant, has moved from his original haunt, which—in a clump of trees by the pond—is a more suitable territory for night-ingales than his present abode on the outskirts of the wood. Usually our bird generations are strictly faithful to one place. For instance, we have had in our garden, ever since we came here, a green woodpecker—or gally bird, as he is called in these parts. The present occupier is at least the third in succession. There have probably been more, but only three that I can positively identify because in each case I have witnessed the catastrophe that brought about the change of landlord.

I shall never forget that cruel day in winter when, glancing across the snow-covered lawn, I saw what looked like a lovely crimson flower lying with its summer green upon the whiteness. I ran to examine it, and found that it was our gally bird. There he lay, as beautiful in death as in life, his beak open and his long tongue hanging piteously like a thread. He must have fallen frozen out of the ash tree on the edge of the lawn, unable to endure this sudden betrayal of his mild south country, its transformation from his own color to alien white.

I bewailed him almost as if he had belonged to me, for I had spent many happy moments watching him hop from post to post in the rose garden or dig for insects in the soil, as tame and friendly as a thrush. I was delighted when that very next summer, at the end of the breeding season, I saw no less than three woodpeckers on the lawn in front of the house. They were quite close to the window, and even field glasses of a very modest range showed them to be two parent birds accompanying a young one. They were digging insects out of the earth and regurgitating them into its beak—at least that is the conclusion that both my husband and I came to after watching them, for I believe it is not known for certain that woodpeckers regurgitate.

They paid several more visits and evidently intended that the young one should settle where they had brought him, for in the end they left him there to fend for himself. All that winter, a mild one, we had the pleasure of watching him flying in and out of a group of poplars, or digging with his long beak only a yard or two from our windows, totally without fear. When spring came he flew away, and in all the yaffle of the woods we liked to think we heard his courting laugh. At the end of the breeding season he was back again, and one could only imagine his adventures in the field of love, for he brought neither wife nor heir. Perhaps he intended to occupy the place himself a bit longer and had established his family in more distant parts.

Alas! he was not long to be the happy landlord. One

morning Joe pointed to something and said: "I reckon that's Maas' Nikolous's work." There quite close to the house lay my poor gally bird with his head eaten off. All round him was the long flowery grass of what in peace-time had been a lawn but which the war had compelled us to "let go." It had been his ruin, for digging for insects in its jungle he had not seen his creeping enemy. All cats are unsympathetic when it comes to birds, but Nickolous is particularly an ogre in this respect. Nest after nest—and I must say that birds build most reck-lessly year after year within his reach—falls to him every spring. In spring he is no longer Nickolous Ridikulous but Nikolous Blunderbore.

Now, I thought, we shall have no more woodpeckers. But I was wrong. A month or two later another—a very young one, his red cap just put on—appeared and oc-cupied the usual territory. Whether he was a son, learn-ing by some mysterious means that his father was dead and the estate unoccupied, who shall say? Anyhow, at the moment of writing he is still in residence, and when summer comes with long grass and a prowling cat we shall do our best to watch over him as he works and plays under our windows. Whether or not these birds are related to one another, they certainly seem to have passed on the legend that we are harmless. Let us hope that this year they have likewise passed on a warning that cats are not.

I confess the inconsistency of hating Nikolous Ridi-kulous for fulfilling his nature in the matter of birds, while encouraging his hunting activities in other direc-tions. He must feel it an injustice to be "good pussy, good cat" when he brings in mice or supports himself for weeks on wild rabbits, but "bad, wicked wretch" when he kills an equally tasty and nourishing bird. I have been told that it is possible to scold cats out of killing birds. I do not believe it. Nikolous certainly knows that he is not supposed to do so, but that does not stop him from doing it. The only result of our scoldings has been that he does not bring his prey into the house, as he brings in mice and rats, but disposes of it in the garden, away from my senseless reactions.

I know I must appear senseless to him (in many other ways besides this) and often I do to myself. Why should I make a fuss about birds that I do not make about mice or rabbits?—equally sensitive and estimable creatures, in fact much more so. For the more I know about birds the more I realize that they have selfish, jealous vindictive natures, greatly inferior to the disposition of the average beast, who is kind and warmhearted in comparison.

Apart from their mates and offspring, they seem to be without generosity or even common decency. They fight their friends and maltreat strangers, they will drive a starving neighbor off a tree thick with more berries than they themselves could possibly eat, they will peck to death the old and sick. They are moral Nazis; from the hen to the robin one sees nothing but aggression, power politics, the rule of terror and of force. Even the bird song which we used to think of as a beautiful expression of love, has now been declared by the naturalists to be no more than a string of threats, the ebullition of the landlord rather than the lover. Any bird's song put into words would not run *Drink to me only with thine eyes* or even *Summer is coming, is coming, I know it, I know it*, but *I'm the king of the castle, get away you dirty rascal*.

So why am I upset when one of these thugs is bumped off? Probably for the same reason that an attractive fraud is nearly always dearer to us than the worthiest of bores. Mice are a bore when they get into the larder and rabbits when they break into the garden, but birds—equally destructive in both should they get the chance—are never a bore, but always beautiful and fascinating to watch. I doubt if Nikolous would accept this excuse for my behavior.

Part V
Pedal Point and Coda

1.

FROM MY WINDOW AS I WRITE I LOOK UP EVERY FEW moments and gaze across a stretch of what once was lawn. It is yellow with buttercups and patched with purple hearts of clover. The oxeyes, which Joe Boorman calls Margaret daisies, are wide open above it on their bronze stalks; the smaller daisies (sewed-a-button daisies) are hidden among spears of waving grass. In my eyes it is all more beautiful than when it was a lawn, than when we scorched the flowers with lawn-sand, and cut the grass to the length of a Victorian convict's hair, and set our friends to work with daisy cutters when they unsuspectingly came to tea.

To most people it is dereliction—"Oh, what a pity you've had to let it go"—and there was a moment, just before it happened, when I too regretted that we had so much grass in our garden plan, so much more than could be mown by an old heavy, obstinate hand mower. Our idea had been to make our garden merge as smoothly as possible into the surrounding countryside. We did not want to gash the fields with civilization, even with the civilization of Eden.

So we made our hedge of "quick" and of the hornbeam which in this part of England is called beech, just as if it were the hedge of a field; and we planted tall Lombardy poplars and ash trees where we wanted shade, and arranged for our flowers to grow in and about stretches of unbroken grass. The lawn, when newly mown, was like a green lake under lovely shadows. There was a strange thrill in stepping on to it from the fields, over the garden stile—a primitive thrill running back to man's first joys of cultivation, when from the exterior roughness he entered the smooth garth of his home-steading.

But it had to go, because we had neither the labor nor the petrol to keep it mown and soon I found that its going was to be no robbery but a new gift. The flowers that had been our enemies became our friends, and all the foreground now is a carpet of them, as lovely in its colors as the grass was in its green. Our scheme, however, for blending with the fieldscape round us has not been improved, because though we are successively a daisy field, a buttercup field, a clover field, a hayfield standing and a hayfield mown, the fields outside have been so incredibly smartened up that we look shaggy by contrast. The step over the stile brings the same change from rough to smooth, but now it is in the opposite direction.

This is not a chapter on gardening. I have no inten-tion of leading any reader up any garden path, for on the subject of gardening I am a heretic. Everything I might be expected to feel in a garden, I feel instead in the kitchen. There I feel happy, confident, interested and soothed—I feel useful and creative. I have never felt anything like this while gardening; planting, weeding, digging, all give me sensations of inefficiency and frus-tration, to which is added an acute bodily discomfort.

Possibly I might enjoy gardening more if it could be done in a vertical position, but there seems no way of remaining upright unless one's garden were to be de-signed like a mountain vineyard, in a series of terraces. In the garden I kneel, stoop or crouch; in the kitchen I sit or stand, except for those few moments when a man-made oven brings me to my knees. In the garden, too, my mind never seems to be really engaged, nor is it ever really free. It moves in circles of irritation round the body's struggle, whereas in the kitchen it is as fully and

·[173]·

gently absorbed in the body's activity as butter in a good sauce.

I do not like gardening, nor am I particularly interested in gardens—in country gardens, that is to say. A town garden is a very different thing. It breaks up the bricks and mortar and provides a refuge from them for the town dweller. It allows him to grow a certain amount of his own goodness and beauty—green peas and sweet peas, leeks and lilies. Its multiplication also makes the beauty of the town. In May and June I am always struck anew by the loveliness of our London suburbs, a loveliness which is almost entirely due to their gardens, for the building and layout as a rule are hideous. A village, too, gains in beauty from the little floral trays which the cottages hold out before them, from the hollyhock and tall delphinium reaching for the thatch. Even a modern bungalow has been redeemed from ugliness by the flowers and trees and bushes that have, while adorning, veiled its ultimate brutalities.

But a well-built house among fields and woods needs no such setting. It must have its kitchen garden and its orchard, and its beds of favorite flowers. But it seems to me that here the complications and elaborations of the British middle-class garden are out of place, and any undue insistence on them will spoil the surrounding beauty only in a smaller degree than aggressive bricks and mortar. For your garden needs to be absorbed by the countryside as well as your house, and a hedge of cupressus—even if alive, and in my experience it is more often dead—looks nearly as awkward beside a chestnut shaw as a pink asbestos roof or a stained-glass window.

I have used the term "middle-class," not in disdain but because the constant talk about gardens and gardening that you hear or used to hear seems to me essentially a middle-class indulgence. I never hear cottage people talking about their gardens—at least not in the same way. Joe Boorman will announce that his potatoes were "freezed" last night or that the mice have "terrified" the spinach, and Mrs. Boorman will point proudly to her

·[174]·

spiklus—a solitary specimen of salpiglossus—but neither holds forth on plans or alterations or tells you how fine their cannas were or are going to be. Also they never move things about—they are far too wise. At the other end of the scale, I do not imagine that dukes and millionaires gossip much together about schemes for replanting the orangery or for transferring the Italian garden from the east to the west side of the lake. It is the people midway between these two groups of garden owners who discuss them so incessantly, and so incessantly emulate and imitate one another that in the end all their gardens seem to be very much alike.

This may sound captious, and I daresay it is; but I have suffered much in the past from garden purists. Once at a luncheon party I sat next an elderly gentleman who spoke of the daisies on my lawn in much the same tone as a district visitor might speak of the bugs in a slum tenement. Another enthusiast had a way of translating into Latin the name of any flower I mentioned and handing it back to me like a schoolmistress returning a corrected exercise. There was also the party in the "Himalayan" garden, where a friend hoarsely whispered to me to hold my tongue because I was upsetting our host by admiring all the wrong things. And even now—after five years of total war—I am still greeted by those whose first wild cry is—"*How* is the garden? Looking lovely, of course!"

It *is* looking lovely, but not in the way they mean—nor is it the way I should mean for peaceful permanence. I like wild gardens, but not untidy ones; there is a distinction. A wild garden follows the lines of nature, with broad spaces and plantings, flowers and trees growing without formal arrangement but in groups conditioned by such natural considerations as soil and slopes and shade. An untidy garden, however, has less of nature in it than of art run to seed. It cries out, like all true art, for elimination, for pruning. My garden, as I see it now, is like one of those vast interminable novels in which nothing is either set in order or left out. The wild flowers in the grass are beautiful in themselves, but they have no artistic unity with the rest; and the flowers in the flower beds wear that air of dereliction which all civilized flowers, especially roses, wear when invaded by the wild.

In a few weeks they will look better. Old Mr. Moon and old Ted Guiver (nobody knows why one is "Mr." and the other just Ted) will come with their scythes, and sweep the wild weedy hay into swathes as regular as if a machine had made them, and nearly as quickly as a machine. They will tell me stories of how this place looked in days far bygone and then they will bring their little old pony to fetch away his winter fodder. At least I hope all this will happen, but from year to year it is precarious; for in a drought our hay may not be worth the carrying, and a wet, springy year means so much hay everywhere that the little old pony may not need ours; and every year makes Mr. Moon and Ted Guiver a little older, a little nearer being reaped instead of reaping.

If they do not come we shall look worse than ever, and if they do we shall not look too good; for a scythed lawn is very different from a mown lawn, and we certainly should not have planned so much green space around us if we had known we should have to depend on the same method as Father Time. . . . Yet how modern and artificial is this distinction. A hundred years ago there were no lawn-mowers in England and every lawn was scythed. The lawns of Buckingham Palace were scythed—the lawns of Pemberley were scythed and the lawns of Mansfield Park; and the lawns (though this will surprise us less) of Brambleton and Booby Hall. We are only going back to the eighteenth century, a time very much more advanced than the barbarism which has necessitated our retreat.

But for better, for worse, the petrol lawn-mower is here, and already I am planning how our desolate places can be restored. For though I do not love gardening I love flowers—indeed, my love of flowers is one reason why I dislike gardening. One reads and hears of the green thumb, the thumb which brings life to every plant it moves and touches. My thumb is a black thumb, and every plant I handle shows its resentment by dying at once. So because I love flowers I have given up handling them. I will rescue them from assaulting weeds and I like arranging them in vases; but I will never interfere with their private, growing lives.

When I was a child my love of flowers was fanatical. Had their beauty been less transient, I should have preferred them to toys. I would do almost anything to obtain the gift of one and my scanty supplies of pocket money often went in their purchase, for we had no garden worthy of the name. We used to pick a certain number of wild flowers in the country; primrosing picnics were among the greatest of the year's treats. But the greatest treat of all was our annual visit to a parsonage garden, where the flowers were not wild, yet were free for my plucking.

To this parsonage every June two elderly ladies came as paying guests. They were patients of my father's, and when he called on them I always drove out with him. They were not particularly attractive old ladies. The elder was very, very old indeed, and the younger, her companion, had no roof to her mouth. I took very little interest in them when they were in their own home; but about them for a single summer month hung all the perfumed glamour of lilac and roses, of jasmine and syringa, irises, peonies, poppies, sweet William and Canterbury bells.

While my father attended the employer, the companion would take the doctor's little girl into the garden, where I was allowed freely and uniquely to pick anything I chose. I remember particularly the little creamy bankshire roses that covered the wall. They were a new experience for me—I had seen them nowhere else; and now when I want them for my own walls they seem to have disappeared from gardeners' catalogues and I am fobbed off with substitutes which are not at all the same thing. The thought arises that they may be very much better, that my bankshire roses are a graft on memory,

[177]

which no nursery man ever created. Creamy roses with golden hearts, pressed tight in sweet-smelling trusses . . . it is possible that my white Dorothy Perkins, while no improvement on what I remember, may be a great improvement on what I actually saw.

I think it must be my memory which has made me such a lover of cheerful, easy flowers—the kind that grow in cottage gardens, always the most generous to a craving child. When we came here I filled the beds with old favorites and bright colors, so that our garden is little more than an extended version of the cottage gardens round us. Uninteresting and unenterprising, says the garden purist; but somehow I cannot bring myself to grow at infinite trouble and expense in half a ton of special manure a tiny blossom the size of a pin's head— even if it be the only specimen outside Afghanistan.

But though I am no gardener, I honor the vocation, which seems to carry with it the relics of man's unfallen state. In the garden he is not only assisting the Creator, but actually developing and improving on His work. As he patiently improves the wild rose with its faint hues and fugitive scent into the glowing colors and heady perfume of a Dame Edith Helen, a Reverend Page Roberts, or an Etoile de Hollande, it looks to me as if he were doing a share of the divine work, a work for which he was originally intended and should now be doing on an infinitely wider, more fruitful, more significant scale.

It is as if God had given man certain ideas and then asked him to improve upon them, as a kindergarten teacher gives a child a mat to embroider with colored wools. I shall be told that wild flowers are as lovely as cultivated flowers, and so no doubt they are in bulk, but not in detail. For their full effect of beauty they depend on masses—sheets of asphodel, carpets of bluebells, clumps of primroses. Is a single bluebell as beautiful as a single hyacinth? Can a single wild lupin, taken from the purple carpet of some Orkney field, compete with a single cultivated spike of Golden Russell? The original wild rhododendron is small and sparsely flowered in comparison with the varieties that man has conceived. In fact every wild flower seems susceptible, by cultivation, fertilization, or grafting, of improvements ahead of its first design.

In this work man has been more honorably successful than in his similar work with the beasts, where he has often followed strange fancies of his own. He has bred horses into nerves and folly, dogs into adenoids and difficult whelping, cats in and out of squints. With flowers he has been less irresponsible, and a garden is still in some measure Eden, though in my own case it is an Eden which bears all too plainly the marks of fallen estate.

I see now that my garden must be made smaller; some of it must be given back to the meadow from which it was originally taken. For though petrol will return to the lawn-mower, I do not expect, or indeed hope for, any adequate return of the labor that pushed that mower over the grass for twelve hours every week. It would be a sorry scandal if the agricultural laborer were once more to be driven out of the fields into the gardens. Nor should I attempt to persuade him—it would be in vain. For the war would have shown me, if I did not know already, how infinitely the countryman prefers field work to garden work, and how reluctantly, and for economic reasons only, he must in those prewar years have given us his collaboration in our long fuss about things-that-do-not-really-matter.

2.

WHEN WE CAME TO LIVE IN THIS HOUSE A FARM laborer, unless highly skilled, could seldom earn more than thirty-five shillings a week, but as a gardener he could be sure of at least two pounds. In consequence farm-workers were glad enough to be taken on as gardeners, and we had a number of applications for the job—not only from farm hands, but from builders' men who, though better paid than the agricultural laborer, were more liable to bouts of unemployment.

Now all that is changed, and agricultural wages are

higher than those paid to most gardeners in these parts. The farmers say they are too high to be economical. They do not seriously contend that three pound ten is more than anyone requires to live on, but they assert roundly that the local farm hand does not really earn it. They point out that the standards of work in a factory are very different from what they are on a farm. The factory pays for the complete use of a man's time while he is working for it. If he idles or dawdles the foreman drops on him; indeed a certain standard of rapidity is required of him by his machine if he is to work at all.

Farm work, on the other hand, is mostly done at the worker's own sweet will. Very few farms in this part of the country run to a foreman and the farmer is generally working too hard himself to be able to supervise his men. Even his best friends would not insist that the Sussex man is a swift worker, and the tempo of our local farms is slow. The work has always been done in a leisurely way, with decent intervals for thought and conversation. There are also the wet days, when the man may do no work at all and yet have to be paid. This was of less importance in former times, when only a few shillings were lost, but nowadays most farmers resent having to pay two men one and threepence an hour for standing all the morning in a barn, talking about Hitler.

It is characteristic of our Sussex workers that they cannot work and talk at the same time, and they are very fond of talking. I have seen Bill Jarman stand motionless as a statue, his shears poised above the hedge he was trimming, while he indulged in earnest conversation with a passer-by. Passers-by were frequent in that lane, and all seemed to be friends of Bill's. I startled my husband by telling him that he owed his employer sixpence.

"Whatever for?"

"For Bill's time. You were talking to him for nearly twenty minutes, during which he never cut a twig. What on earth were you talking about?"

"Lunatics."

"Which lunatics?"

"Oh, none especially—merely lunatics in general. He's interested in lunatics."

So when payday comes the piper has to pay for Bill Jarman's little chat with my husband on lunatics, as well as probably a dozen others equally entertaining—to say nothing of such distractions as chasing Mrs. Larkin's dog out of the field, showing a linnet's nest to Tommy Trout, or helping Mrs. Boorman repack her shopping bag after the last tin had burst it. This might not have mattered so much in the bad old days of fifteen, or even of thirty shillings a week, but it upsets the economic balance of the farm if in order to finish his hedge Bill Jarman has to be put on overtime at one and ninepence an hour.

Even in the bad old days it must sometimes have been thought that too much time was wasted, for there is a strong tradition of piecework in these parts. We have living in our cottages Tom Borrer a stout admirer of the bad old days—or good old times, as he prefers to call them. We had paid thirteen pounds to have a trench dug for an electric cable.

"When my father was a boy you could have got that done at fivepence an ell."

A hasty calculation showed at that rate the trench would have cost us about thirteen shillings and we eagerly assured him that we were willing to take him on at any time at his father's wages. He did not, however, avail himself of the offer; but when, some months after the war had started, we engaged him to "lay along" a hedge, he insisted on being paid at piece rates.

We made inquiries as to what these were, for we gathered that even he had abandoned the ideal of fivepence an ell. But nobody could tell us—neither the War Agricultural Committee, nor the Farmers' Union, nor any local employer. No one had paid for piecework since before the last war, and there were no official rates.

This did not, however, discourage our reactionary and he himself suggested that he should do the job for five pounds. We accepted gladly, for we imagined that this would galvanize him into frenzies of speed and give us our hedge in a week. Nothing of the sort. All that happened at the end of the week was that Joe Boorman who worked with him at the normal wage, was paid four pounds, while he received two pounds ten. This so surprised and distressed him that we had not the heart to hold him to his bargain and he finished the hedge a fortnight later, having paid no more than thirty shillings for his love of the past.

3.

THERE CAN BE FEW PARTS OF BRITAIN MORE temperamentally conservative than this little southeastern parish within sixty miles of London. Or rather I should say that few parts of Britain maintain so high a proportion of horny, hard-bitten reactionaries in their general population. The local attitude, I fear, is based more on an unthinking attachment to familiar ways than on any really intelligent valuation of the past. We vote for our member of Parliament not so much because we approve of his political views, if any, as because we voted for him at the last election when we voted for him because we had voted for him at the one before, and so on back to the days when our father voted for him in 1902. Not until the habit is broken by his death or resignation will we vote for anyone else.

Reaction is unfashionable at the moment, but there is already a shadow of its return. Discriminating lovers of the past are no longer afraid to confess a nostalgia for the eighteenth century, if intellectuals, or for the twelfth, if Catholics. People in general are beginning to suspect that reaction need not be wholly to past abuses any more than all advance is inevitably toward a brave new world. We certainly need a few dead weights like Tom Borrer, to ballast the perhaps too lightly laden craft of our progress through unknown, stormy seas.

We shall advance very much more steadily, if not perhaps more quickly, if we accept the fact that the past is still with us, that it cannot be emptied away like bilge water. To change the metaphor, it must be taken into consideration in any future that is to be a concrete three-dimensional reality and not a mere two-dimensional blue-print that never comes to life.

Reaction has its banes as well as its blessings, but so has progress, and personally I should find it difficult to choose between them, though, again personally, I find reactionaries less tiring to live with than undiluted progressives. This may be deplorable, but the last few years have shown me the virtues and advantages of such men as Tom Borrer in a way that they have not shown similar qualities in their opposites.

The main virtue of the conservative mind, its chief, most honorable sublimation, is loyalty. The man who cannot be shaken out of his habits is not easily shaken out of his attachments. Perhaps, you say, his attachments are habits, in which case all I can say is that, if they are, in this case they are good ones. His attachment to the place where he was born, to the soil, to his employers, to his home, all stand for something which is passing away in some quarters but should not be allowed to pass away.

I am pleased to think that the old Sussex ways of speech can still be found within sixty miles of London and not only on the lips of the old. It is a better speech than any learned at school—older, richer, spicier, plummy with words that Shakespeare used. Joe Boorman is still in his thirties, but nearly every time I talk to him I go away enriched with some savory morsel that I taste for the next hour.

I can forgive him for "not troubling" to pick the mushrooms he knows I want in the kitchen, when he tells me that I can find them still growing "in de li'l nooket whur de harrow (pronounced to rhyme with Faro) lays," and cheerfully watch the bad weather spoil my afternoon when he has foretold it from a "scrutty" moon or from the big clouds he calls "Hastings ladies." I can even bear the failure of my espaliered apple trees if he refers to their harvest as "scrumps."

Tom Borrer calls the Great Bear "Jack and His Waggon," while Orion is the "Kite," and other constellations have homely names that I prefer to those found for them either by the Greeks or by Mr. H. P. Herbert. Old Fuggle tells me that the pullets will soon be in lay, because they have begun to prate. Their feeding trough he rhymes with throw, and their mashes are their pats. Like Milton's, all our autumn leaves are sere; and we have practically no present participles—we do not say "it is raining" but "it rains," indeed sometimes it rains hard enough to knock a dog over.

Sunny weather is a "butterfly day," a drought is a "drythe," and when the rain's lost we "go to look for it in the north." None of these are Sussex dictionary words and phrases, but they are in general use round here on the Kentish border, together with many survivals of French Huguenot occupation. The lodge (shed) or the grate may be equally "in dishable," our hens scratch corn out of the "grattans" or autumn stubble fields, our place names such as Marsh Quarter, Peening Quarter, Upper Quarter retain the *quartier* of the old French acreage, which also survives in the strange verb "to cater," meaning to walk or ramble—possibly from the habit of measuring an acre by so many paces.

I shall be sorry if and when this old way of speaking dies. It has nothing but instinctive conservatism to keep it alive—neither remoteness from London nor the silence of other tongues, which hour after hour pour their emasculated English into the microphone. Nor has Sussex been kept alive, like Yorkshire or Lancashire, on the stage. It is a soft, slurry speech and does not come well across the footlights, though it has been remarkably audible and effective on the wireless when sung by Buttercup Joe.

Already the women, who always adapt themselves more quickly than men to new ways, good or bad, are giving it up; and a curious lady's maid language is taking its place in certain quarters, a genteel compromise, blown out with spurious aspirates. I once had a cook who, though she had many surviving Sussex phrases in her speech, would have thought it very unrefined to call a hegg an egg.

But many Sussex women with new ways of speech follow old ways of living. Many of them still prefer the duck's nest grate to a modern oil cooker—cookery by gas or electricity, even if available, is too expensive for the farm laborer's wife. They use kitchen physic rather than modern proprietory medicines, they shop in their own village rather than in the neighboring town; and they continued to brew wines until sugar rationing made it impossible.

Sussex was—and I hope again will be—a grand place for wines. In addition to the more usual kinds, such as dandelion, gooseberry, elderberry and the delicious elder-flower, the most unlikely vegetables have been conscripted into the bacchanalian ranks. Peas, beans, turnips, parsnips, potatoes, have given the struggling farm hand his moments of glory and oblivion—for like most home-made wines our Sussex wines are remarkably potent and have been the downfall of many who have taken them lightly.

I find my own taste spoiled by a long experience of continental wines. If I had not drunk so much wine made from grapes I probably should not, as I do, feel my palate outraged by such a basis as plum. My dear old friend, Mrs. Cramp, topped in easier times her deep measure of childhood's memories by sending me every Christmas the most excellent bottle of plum wine; and by the time I had finished it I was enjoying it. The first glass or two inevitably suggested a claret that had "gone off."

It is sad that wine can no longer be made at home, for the Sussex workingman really enjoys it and is a connoisseur within the rather peculiar range of his tastes and materials. I know a woodman who always had a mug of wine every evening before his tea as a sort of cocktail—so potent that even to sniff it made me feel giddy. He must miss it sorely now, for local vintages (or rather plummages or turnipages) do not admit of long keeping—

becoming explosive at an early date. And though I have heard of a "cellar" of five hundred bottles kept by a local thatcher, the usual custom is to drink the bottle within the year before it blows the cork out.

4.

THESE GOOD TRADITIONS OF WORDS AND WINE ARE ONLY external constancies, perhaps more picturesque than really admirable. It is in the fundamental constancy of his nature that the Sussex man shows the finest quality of reaction. During the war this constancy came into its own. It was particularly valuable in the ups and downs, rapids and torpids, of civil defense. In the Army I admit that the typical son of Sussex must have been a constant source of grief and irritation to his drill sergeant. In fact I was once told that this was so well known by the authorities that it was the custom to disperse Sussex farm hands as widely as possible among less resistant material from other counties. In action there could be few braver, and none more stubborn, but on the barrack square a squad of Sussex rookies must have been the heart break of any officer who valued appearances (the voice of Tom Borrer rising scornfully from a past altercation—"Well, of course if you want that flower bed to *look* nice I ain't got nothing to say").

But in those other services, whose war motto might have been "They also serve who only stand and wait" the Sussex man came into his own. None better than he at standing and waiting. In many parts of England a long period of inaction would mean either the mizzling away of the personnel (unhappy word that has escaped from italics and inverted commas into the freedom of our language) or its deterioration into grouses and squabbles. Even in this district those departments of A.R.P. mainly run and staffed by the "gentry" were more liable to disintegration in the course of a lull than those supported by the working classes.

For some reason in our village fire fighting was not considered a genteel form of civil defense; and whereas almost every sort of gentleman and (more prevalently) gentlewoman appeared at one time to be some sort of air raid warden, the fire service had been left to democratic initiative, which in our part of the world confines itself mainly to whist drives. As a result, though the place was crowded with wardens, sub-wardens, nurses, ambulances, rescue squads and gas squads, the positions of the various fire hydrants were unmarked and unknown, and when at last they were found some were also found to have been buried under concrete.

It fell to my husband to organize our local Auxiliary Fire Service, so I had plenty of opportunity for hearing of and sometimes seeing Joe Boorman, Tom Borrer, and their friends in action. I have also seen them in inaction, when their special genius found its richest expression.

In the summer and autumn of 1940, our village A.F.S. team saw more active service than any other local department of civil defense. Our fields had their share of wrecked planes, including, alas! some of the defending Few. The main concern of our boys was with these and secondarily with burning crops and woods. In a neighborhood where the houses are scattered, even in the villages, there could not be many domestic fires, but when bombs fell the fire service came to be reckoned as a sort of auxiliary rescue squad, as its methods of mobilization and travel brought it into action more swiftly than any other department.

The A.F.S. soon became exceedingly popular, not only in the parish but throughout the rural district. Manual-pump parties and stirrup-pump parties formed themselves as readily as whist tables, besides those more proudly grouped round a Coventry Climax. Every night Sussex laboring men who had worked all day in the fields or on local defenses repaired to barns and stables hurriedly adapted for uncomfortable sleeping, and there spent the night in cots (if so be they had managed to wring them out of the costiveness of official stores) or on deck chairs or whatsoever decayed, unwanted furniture their wives could lend them. There they slumbered round the pump and sometimes the telephone—though for the latter they had often to rely on being rung up at Mus' So-and-So's.

Many such nests were found when the N.F.S. swallowed up the A.F.S. in 1941: little groups of men—cowmen, stockmen, hedgers, hop driers, roadmen, builders' men—in lonely villages and six-house hamlets, who had had scarcely any training and had never been called out to any fire, who nevertheless had slept perseveringly out of their beds in cold and discomfort, ignored by the authorities but sustained by the thought that some day their country might need them. It was with the deepest disappointment that they accepted their demobilization and handed over their stirrup pumps to the newly organized Fire-Watchers.

In the towns firemen had to be "managed," propitiated, placated, occupied and entertained if nothing much was happening. Not so the countrymen. The section my husband raised in 1939 lasted virtually till the end of the war, though affected by such irresistible external forces as the army call-up and the reorganization under the N.F.S.

It also lost its two firewomen. These joined as telephonists in 1940, and for two years they shared on alternate nights the men's vigils in the dark, shambling garage behind the village shop. Not one single night's duty did they miss, though one of them had to come a considerable distance and both worked hard during the day. A fireman might backslide or be kept away by external causes, but nothing prevented either Mrs. Adis or Miss Coven from being at the telephone, where she sat like a wraith under the shaded light, beside the sleeping men.

At first the telephonist kept vigil all night (so these two women slept on alternate nights only); but when an edict went forth from headquarters, that no telephonist was to be on duty for more than two consecutive hours, she had to give up her monopoly and take her turn with the men. Instead of sitting beside them on her chair at the old card table which supported the telephone and the occurrence book she slept in her own cot in the row of cots—a cot made up for her most punctiliously every night by the firemen who slept in the others. And if you think that rather an odd arrangement, I can only say that no one else thought so and that it worked admirably, causing neither friction in the fire station nor scandal in the village.

Our village is not very prominent on the map and it was some time after the A.F.S. and the old fire brigade had been amalgamated under the National Fire Service that anyone troubled to come and inspect our fire station. But when at last somebody came from headquarters and discovered the sleeping arrangements everything began to happen at once.

The firewomen were told that they must on no account come on night duty until they had been provided with separate quarters. As the station was now manned only at night this meant their complete suspension while a swarm of builders descended on the premises and divided and subdivided them, partitioned and repartitioned them till they seemed to have nearly as many compartments as an egg box. In the old days of action the firemen had slept beside their pump. Now they had a messroom (which would never be used, as the station was shut by day) and a kitchen as well as sleeping quarters and a proper garage. But when all the tumult and the shouting had died and the commanders and the column officers departed, there was still no accommodation for the women telephonists. Their sleeping quarters had been forgotten.

The days before all this happened are still referred to by the local firemen as "the good old days." Not only were they days of fellowship and freedom, before the Army had taken away some of the best of the boys and bureaucracy driven out the girls, but they were days of action, when they felt themselves of national importance, manning a pump in a suburb of Hell's Corner, taking their share of excitement and danger both in their own village and in more perilous places—as when they were sent as "relief" into the chaos of the Portsmouth and London blitzes. From this they now had turned to be paid, whole-time firemen, exiled to Hastings or Eastbourne or Rye, or other foreign parts, at least ten miles from home, or to be part-timers, doing biweekly duty only in a village of no importance, where nothing ever happened any more. A smaller deterioration would have earned the epithet "good old" for the days that used to be.

It was to those "good old days" that I owe the discovery of one of my greatest kitchen comforts—the *bain-marie*. My problem then was how to feed my husband, for he had to go on duty at every alert, and sometimes we had as many as eight alerts a day, generally at meal-times. The "alarm" as it was called at that period always sounded just as he was sitting down to his breakfast or his dinner or his supper. It was quite possible for him to have nothing all day besides cups of tea and those little presents of food the kind villagers took into the fire station. This did not worry him much, but it worried me, and the rather scatterbrained cook I had at the time was no help at all. It was Mrs. Boorman who remembered that old Nellie had had a much better way of coping with delayed and interrupted meals than putting the dishes to stand and dry up in the oven.

The *bain-marie* did not, however, solve all our catering problems during the Battle of Britain; for my husband perhaps might not come home till another meal was due, to have that snatched from him by the telephone with its "AIR RAID MESSAGE—RED," just as he was going to sit down. The complete solution came from the actual disturber of our peace. It was on very simple lines, but we did not think of it for ourselves. An army officer pointed out to me that Jerry came over at pretty much the same time every day. "Why don't you alter the time of your meals to suit him?" We did, and we were able to finish many more of them. Indeed, the new timetable

·[190]·

turned out, for other reasons, to be so much more convenient than the old one that we have stuck to it ever since.

5.

I HAVE NEVER BEEN ABLE TO FIND IN WRITING THE escape from external things that I find in cooking. Cooking takes my mind off everything but itself, for the reason that I am not a seasoned cook and therefore have to think and concentrate. At the same time this concentration is effortless—unlike the concentration involved in literary work, which is so very effortful that if there be any real opposition from outside I can make no headway against it. There is, too, also in writing an emotional drain which can eventually bring about complete exhaustion; but in cooking, fatigue is bodily and passes away with rest.

This surprises me a little, because I am the reverse of that active, resourceful type which, while ill at ease in mental and spiritual spheres, finds a natural outlet in the practical and physical. Neither am I in the least "domesticated." In all the mixed ingredients of my nature, I should say that the quantity of "Martha" is very much less than the quantity of "Mary." I am by nature absent-minded, forgetful, and incompetent in my dealings with inanimate objects, especially if these are attached to any sort of mechanical or electrical device of which I have a positive fear. In my cooking I am perpetually struggling against these limitations—and yet I enjoy it.

It is true that some dreadful things have happened. I have poured a saucepan of hot water into the middle of a spongecake, and wildly emptied a whole week's ration of sugar into a small quantity of stewed fruit. I also find myself forever on the verge of producing Hamlet without the Prince of Denmark, for if I forget to put in any ingredient it is always the principal one. But, up to the time of writing, let me boast that I have retrieved all my disasters without loss. Only one concoction of mine has gone uneaten into the hen pail, and that was a dish correctly made according to a Ministry of Food recipe. (No doubt the vitamins were all assembled in their proper strength but the flavor was revolting.) In the case of the spongecake, after a little draining and stirring, it turned into a very passable Madeira, and the stewed blackberries became some of the most delicious jam I have tasted. As for Hamlet, I have hitherto always remembered him just in time, and "the stage waits" has had no permanent effect on the production.*

I have little doubt but that at the back of my cooking exists a creative impulse which make the difficulties worth while. Other mugs have found the same, but I do not think that it necessarily involves a genius for cookery any more than the widespread urge to write means that all who feel it will be even moderately successful. It certainly does not always go with other types of domesticability. I have friends whom the shortage of domestic help has revealed as enthusiastic housemaids, but to whom cooking is nothing but a bore. Other friends can do anything with a needle and very little with a saucepan. Indeed I find that for the average "domesticated" female cooking takes second place, possibly because the average woman is not really interested in food as food. She cooks for her household, and for their sakes and her own is anxious to cook well, but if she is alone she troubles very little. "Bread and onions" and "a lettuce in the bathroom" are two lone-female menus I can vouch for. The latter is full of provocative suggestion.

Men, on the other hand, if they cook at all, are deeply concerned with it and generally cook very well indeed.

* This is not, however, always necessary, as Mrs. Doris Grant has shown in *Your Daily Bread*. The fact that she had been making bread for six months before she realized that she had left out what most people would consider, the most important part of the process —i.e., the kneading—makes my heart go out to her as a true sister cook. While her discovery (which I have confirmed) that wholemeal bread is very much better for not being kneaded makes me wonder what Mr. John Gielgud and Mr. Donald Wolfit might do if they chose.

A man who would be a perfect mug at cleaning the house will sometimes in the kitchen show himself both efficient and inspired—which reinforces the notion that any form of creative impulse, even in a female, is essentially male. Man is the creator, the originator, while woman preserves and maintains. Ordinary housework is one long orgy of maintenance, the preservation of something already there. In cooking, however, something is continually being made, not out of nothing but out of a variety of other things, often very unlike itself. In this way it resembles all creative art, and more widely, all constructive thought. So perhaps it is not so very mysterious that imaginative unpractical natures should find in it an affinity. Mary may, after all, have been a better cook than Martha. . . .

6.

"LORD, SPEAK TO MY SISTER."
That prayer is often in my heart, but the sister concerned is Martha. I pray to be delivered from Martha, from her interruptions and irruptions, from her bursting into my moments of recollection. The Mass is not yet half over, but Martha is already telling me that it is time I mixed the batter for the Yorkshire pudding— "It ought to stand at least an hour." Or she suddenly shouts: "Have you remembered to write that list for the Army and Navy Stores? . . . No? . . . Well, there's a pencil in your handbag. You had better do it now, or you will forget it entirely." Mary tries hard to cling to her "better part," but there is for some reason about Martha the bustling voice of conscience, and the distractions she provides have a moral urgency lacking in the normal run of distractions during Mass.

"Lord, speak to my sister."

These two sisters have become symbols. In actual fact they are saints of the Church, inspired by different though not contrary virtues; but symbolically they divide the human race. I write as a child of Mary, voicing my complaint against the children of Martha, whom Kipling has championed on grounds that seem to me mistaken. Certainly he has misunderstood her story. When she interrupted the conversation between her Guest and her sister with the demand that it should cease forthwith and Mary devote herself instead to her assistance, she was showing herself, it seems to me, an indifferent hostess—one of the type which will not allow her company to enjoy itself in its own way.

For her, no doubt, the meal she was preparing was the most important part of the entertainment, and she could not allow for a different taste. We are told that she was "cumbered about"—a graphic phrase—and "careful about many things." But it would be wrong to picture her as an overworked housewife in the modern British style, drudging and struggling while her sister loafed. An oriental household such as hers would have been full of servants and her activities mainly those of supervision and organization. No, it seems to me that she was being fussy and overanxious, and perhaps a little resentful of the detachment of her sister and her Guest. Her halo is not made of the stuff of that awkward moment.

Mary, on the other hand, has not had her due from those who take no account of official halos. They regard her as a pious dreamer, too selfish and lazy to do her plain duty. I have even heard her reproached for waiting in the house when Christ came to visit it on the death of Lazarus, and Martha characteristically rushed out to meet Him, "but Mary sat at home." They ignore the fact that it was Mary, not Martha, who attended her Lord through all the dangers and horrors of the Crucifixion. She sat at home when the welcoming crowd ran out to meet Him, but when the mob cried, "Crucify him! Crucify him!" she ran to be at His side. I can picture Martha comforting the bereaved Apostles with her hospitality, but Mary who once sat at home is now among the soldiers and the mob at the foot of the Cross. This timid, spineless creature is exposing her body to danger

·[194]·

and her soul to the utmost grief. It is she, too, and not Martha, who is to be engaged in the unpleasantly practical business of embalming the body which had been hastily put into the grave on the eve of the last Sabbath.

Of course to those whose ideas of holiness are still Victorian in shape, the traditional identification of Mary of Bethany with Mary of Magdala is something almost shocking. Yet there is nothing wrong with it in psychology or in experience. It is an error to think that it is always the good girl of the family who becomes a nun—it is just as likely to be her "difficult" sister. The contemplative life needs qualities of concentration and self-donation which, if turned in the wrong direction, might well lead to the streets of Magdala. Useful, bustling Martha has an outlet for her temperament in every small concern, in every passing moment of the day, but the Mary type—reflective, interior, inactive, introverted, call it what you will—cannot escape through these small archways. It demands a wider exit into love or into religion, and we can imagine Martha's sister making her first escape into love. It is just as easy to imagine the disillusion, the growing disgust of such a nature with its own choice—the conflict, the revulsion, and the final liberation when seven devils are cast out.

History is full of similar examples, from St. Augustine to Charles de Foucauld, from Lais of Corinth through Teresa of Avila to Eve de Lavallière. No, I cannot see any psychological difficulty, but I certainly see a social one. I find it difficult to picture a converted harlot in a Jewish household of the first century. According to tradition, Martha and Mary belonged to a rich and noble family, and they seem to have been respected citizens of Bethany. When Lazarus died their home was full of mourning neighbors and there does not appear to be any sign of social ostracism and only one individual expression of Pharisaic contempt.

On the other hand, the constitution of the family is peculiar by the standards of its age and race. Two unmarried sisters living with an unmarried brother must surely have been a remarkable phenomenon in early Palestine. It belongs rather to our own times, and its existence in those suggests some unusual circumstance. Have I leave to conjecture Bethany as a sort of Little Gidding, where a brother and two sisters live a semiconventual life, sharing all three in the repentance and reparation of the "woman who was a sinner" but now has "chosen that better part"?

Certainly the household of Bethany loses much of its life if we exclude Mary Magdalen and reduce it to two flat opposites. Only a second-rate novelist will mold a character as a consistent type. Most of us are compounded just as antithetically as those two Marys. Indeed most of us have Martha thrown in as well, and life is one long conflict between the three.

"Lord, speak to my sister". . . .

7.

IT IS NOTICEABLE THAT THE LORD DID NOTHING OF THE kind. Nor, if I may reverently make such a conjecture, would He have "spoken" to Martha, had the protest been on Mary's side, had she complained that the fuss and clatter of Martha's serving interfered with her spiritual concentration. My conjecture is based on His earlier pronouncement that "wisdom is justified of all her children."

This phrase surely expresses the whole secret of toleration. Or rather it gives it a much wider base than toleration usually has. Nowadays at its best it stands for little more than putting up with the other man's deficiencies because it would be bad manners to interfere, and at its worst for mere indifference.

We pride ourselves on being more tolerant than our fathers, but I doubt if we are any such thing. It is only the grounds of our intolerance that have shifted. We are just as intolerant in the political field as our ancestors were in matters of religion. Religion no longer shines so brightly that we are dazzled, and blind to any light save that which blinds us; but politics—or rather, ideologies —do. Three hundred years ago it would have required all the moral courage I possess and probably much more, to avow myself a Catholic, whereas now it would require the same quality to avow myself a Fascist—which I nervously add that I am not. I am as anxious to escape any undeserved suspicion of that kind as a decent sixteenth century citizen would be to avoid the suspicion of popery. The results in each case would probably be the same—contempt, distrust, social ostracism, if not imprisonment without trial.

All this makes me feel a little out of place, for I have no political or ideological emotions. Fascism and Communism both affect me in the same way. They both seem equally to consist in the diversion of the religious instinct into social and political channels. In each case the state takes the place of God and the Kingdom of Heaven falls to earth with a sickening thud. I see in neither any real chance for freedom, individuality, art or inspiration. The whole of life becomes metallic and set in a mold. Humanity no longer walks or runs, still less skips or dances—in spite of people's parks and Strength through Joy—but marches, marches, marches . . . left, right—left, right . . . the jungle drum is back again, beating a new version of its old rhythm, in squares and sports palaces, in the press and on the radio, a voice that has sound but no meaning, that has rhythm but no tune.

At home our politics are less sinister, but not more inspiring, And again they are all the same. What is the difference between a Labor and Conservative government in power? Bureaucracy comes down on each like a rubber stamp and obliterates anything individual it may have written on the parliamentary page when it was out of office. Just as well, says the cynic; that is the way we keep this country quiet and comfortable when every other country is burning and blowing up. But it is very difficult to feel intolerant under such conditions.

But perhaps that would not matter so much if one did not also feel uninterested. For any large proportion of a country to be uninterested in politics amounts to a national disaster. It was mainly because so many good and intelligent people in France had held aloof from politics, or rather from *ces sales politiciens qui nous empoisonnent la vie* (as I once heard them described by a responsible citizen), that the country came to grief in 1940. For too long good and intelligent people had stood apart from the mess, shrugging their shoulders and letting it seep into the Army, the Navy, and all the main departments of national life except the Church. In Britain our politics are not dirty, but they are dull, because so often burning questions are quenched into a compromise that pleases nobody. There is also the fact —at least I am prepared to argue that it is a fact—that our present electoral system is not truly representative. It expresses only in the vaguest way the real wishes and opinions of the man and woman in the street.

I have had a vote ever since votes were given to women, but I have never voted wholeheartedly, because never have I felt at any time that any candidate represented *me*. My present member of Parliament is without doubt an excellent and worthy man, but he is not likely ever to say or do anything that I would say or do in his place. He does not appear to care twopence for my real interests, which are not so very unlike those of the thousands of other women who have voted him and then longed to kick him in the pants. If I write to him, either in protest or petition, he sends me a printed postcard telling me that the matter is receiving his attention, which means that it has gone into his wastepaper basket.

I have been told that the only way to have a grievance noticed is to write to the *Times*, upon which the Ministry concerned will come tumbling over your M.P.'s head to get the matter hushed up. But in that case, why bother about a vote?

The fact is that I should have an author to represent

me, a farmer should have a farmer, and doctors a doctor, and engineers an engineer, till the House of Commons becomes a vast Rotary Club. Somebody sniffs and says that would be the corporative state . . . Fascism . . . Fe, Fi, Fo, Fum . . . to which I reply that it seems a pity that such a truly democratic plan should hitherto have been tried out in Fascist countries only. Geographical representation is all very well if the part of the country represented is self-contained and the member a genuine inhabitant. It is a farce for a stranger to come down to Little Muddlecombe from London and ask for the division's vote on the sole strength of his being a Socialist—or a Liberal—or a Conservative, while having at best only an acquired and sketchy knowledge of his constituency's needs.

I am not suggesting that petty local interests should take precedence of national planning (as happened in an early Rye election, when the program of both candidates centered on the question of repairs to the Landgate clock), but I suggest that the representative of a trade, profession or guild is more genuinely representative of his constituency than the representative of a set of people held together only by arbitrary politico-geographical boundaries.

There is no use arguing with me, for I am convinced beforehand that the system would not work. Canvassing and elections would both have to be conducted through the post, and once Parliament was assembled the party system would be at an end, because one day the dentists and the doctors might vote with the farmers and the engineers and another day they might vote against them. It would always be a case of individual responsibility, of weighing each question on its own merits, of personal initiative and private information. It would work only in a country where everybody thinks or where nobody thinks at all. In this country, where the art of herd thinking has reached such perfection, it would be a setback to democracy. We should find ourselves compelled to think separately, and the loss of interest in politics would become a general instead of an exceptional discontent. As a nation we have always loved party politics—loved them so dearly that it matters little if the parties under their war paint are really all the same. In countries where the parties are fundamentally opposed, the situation is different, and I only hope that our zeal for party government will not turn us into its missionaries throughout an already sufficiently unquiet world.

But, as I have said, this is not a subject on which I can bring myself to think or feel very strongly. I am wrong, because I make myself like those Frenchmen of the 1930's who when the floods were rising turned their backs and puffed smoke rings. Nor am I a really tolerant person. Like many people, I am intolerant in small matters. I can agree with my adversary very well on grand affairs of politics and religion, but I find it much more difficult to get on with him if he wants to shut the window when I want it open.

In this I think I am behaving in an especially female manner. I have noticed that many women have a tendency to invest the smaller issues of life with a sort of moral significance which is invisible to the average male. I have heard a woman speak of friends who expected (in peacetime) what she called a "meat breakfast" in tones that could not have been more damning had they expected gin instead of early tea. A friend who dislikes onions always conveys the idea that onions are morally reprehensible, and I know another woman whose contempt of lentils has produced in me such a guilt complex that I have made them, as far as she is concerned, a private addiction. The controversy between tea and coffee, too, sometimes echoes former asperities between unionists and home-rulers.

As for myself, I find my main intolerance to lie in matters of temperament. I fall too easily into an attitude of moral indignation against those who differ from my personal tastes in their emotional and mental make-up. I like people who are capable without being energetic,

I like people whose affections are strong, but sentimentality makes me feel sick and sadistic. I like people to have wit and humor, but I hate them to be merry and bright. I am ill at ease with those whose life has no religious depths, but equally ill at ease with those whose life is all depths, without any temporal surface to skip on. I am shy of those who have no "nerves" but are afraid only of strictly legitimate perils. I flee in terror from those who would be mentally or physically intimate.

These are my personal tastes and distastes and I have a right to them. Where I am wrong is in attaching blame and contempt to those who gush or sparkle, slop or flop, or who entertain the fish queue with their own private solution of the riddle of the universe. We are all guilty. Those of us who are quick in thought and action grow impatient with the careful, deliberate steps of the slow-minded, while these believe that our failures are one and all due to the speed of our undertakings, The introvert chills and repels the extrovert, who in his turn fills the introvert and embarrassed boredom. The intellectual is only too ready to despise the simple-minded, who counters with a hearty derision of all high-brows. Nervous people think nerveless people are either swanking or made of leather, and the nerveless people are all agreed that the nervous could "help it if only they tried." From us all rises the prayer—"Lord, speak to my sister—change her spots to my stripes," ignoring the fact that the Lord who made the tiger made the leopard too.

If there is one beauty which the divine Artist seems to have spread more widely than another in His creation it is the beauty of variety. *Circumdata de Varietate*, says the Vulgate of the robe of the King's daughter— "surrounded with variety." And certainly (if I may so express myself) there is no more uncommon thing in nature than two things which are the same. Sameness, regimentation, mass production, these are all manifestations of the enemy—of Satanic interference with mankind and his development. Any sort of totalitarian

civilization, whether the state be represented by a dictator or more insidiously by a bureaucracy, produces,
systematizes and establishes these evils, crushing together
Martha and Mary in one soulless identity. The Lord
will not speak to your sister, but the Führer will.

8.

DO I REALLY APPROVE, THEN, OF PEOPLE BEING AND
doing exactly as they please? I have a terror of
forcing any man's mind in religion, and I have proclaimed myself allergic to politics. I know I am intolerant in small matters, but at the same time I
acknowledge in this my obvious lack of piety and wisdom.
Is there any point in which I should with a good conscience enjoy seeing the state interfere with private
lives—a new point where it does not interfere already?
I am not thinking of crime, but of various crimeless
enterprises which I cannot believe are for the common
good.

The first one that comes into my mind is the spoiling
of our rural districts by suburban intrusions and senseless, disorganized building. I have seen too much of this
during my life, for I have always lived in a part of the
country easily accessible from London and more than
ordinarily agreeable in its climate and natural beauty.
I have also lived to see farming sink to an economic
level when often the only way to keep at least a part of
the farm going was to sell off some other part to a
speculative builder. I have seen big estates broken up
and destroyed for agriculture as well as for beauty by
money-making syndicates. I have seen hard-working
people lose their savings and fill the end of their lives
with care and disappointment owing to the unchecked
activities of a rural housing racket which is well inside
the law.

The various town planning acts have done a little
good, but not so much as they might. No clause seems

to be built without an escape hatch, and the administrative conditions are too complicated and hazy for rigorous enforcement. Also the whole matter is bound up with the state of farming. No prosperous farmer who is not also insane will sell the road frontage of his best field for the erection of shoddy bungalows; on the other hand, a farmer struggling in a coil of tithe, taxation, rising costs and falling prices, would have a just grievance if he might not retrieve his fortunes by selling a few acres to the only person who will buy—the builder.

All this must be considered apart from the housing shortage, which this type of building has in the past done little to remedy. The retired city man or tradesman, the artist and weekender, have found homes of a sort while the agricultural laborer still goes unhoused. The genuine countryman has seen his home and his livelihood depart as farm after farm is sold into the same degradation—the house "modernized," (which in most cases means made to look so ancient that its survival is a cause of wonder) while the land goes derelict, either being sold off in plots or blackmailed on to the purchaser of the farmhouse with the threat of building. That fields "go back" if not regularly dredged and rolled, that hedges sprout and sprawl into jungles if left unbrushed, are facts of rural life unknown to those who have apparently never heard of the curse of Eden. For the last twenty years the country has enjoyed a ghastly boom in the wrong quarters, with the result that the wrong people have come to live in it, people who do not really understand country life and only imagine that they love it.

For such people I have no tolerance. Against such people I should like to legislate. Indeed I should like to make it impossible for anyone to live in the country who could not pass a simple examination of fitness. We have made our roads less dangerous by imposing a test on motorists, so why should we not protect our matchless countryside by having a test for every townsman who thinks he hears the call of the wild?

·[203]·

The first question would be: "Why do you want to live in the country?" That, I think, would disqualify a number of the candidates at the start. Many people decide to live in the country on the strength of a summer car trip, and realize when winter comes that it would have been a kindness to have stopped them. Others want to go rustic because they have been led up the garden path in a popular book. Some choose the country because they think it is cheaper than the town. They are right—it is; and I should pass them on that question while wanting to ask several others.

Those who come into the country to farm should certainly be put to a further searching inquiry. How much do they know about farming? Have they ever farmed before or known anyone who has a commercial farm? How much land have they and what do they propose to do with it? Are they fond of animals? (disqualified if they say yes). If they mean to engage labor, will it be an experienced countryman or their Cousin George, who has never had a job, poor dear, since he lost his clerkship in the Brazen Assurance Company?

If all this is answered satisfactorily, the examination passes on to more trivial matters. Will you patronize the local shops or buy everything, even your eggs and fruit, in the nearest town? How often will you want to visit that town in the course of a month? How long can you live without the cinema? Will you walk through the fields in gloves? If your hens do not lay, whose fault will you think it—theirs or yours? Will you subscribe to the District Nursing Association or concentrate your charitable impulses on an ambulance that will take you into the town should you ever be ill enough to claim its services? Will you undertake in any emergency to call in the village policeman and not send over his head for his superiors, even if he is obliged, like the skipper of the "Hesperus," to have his little daughter bear him company when he comes to dissuade your cook from cutting your throat with the vegetable knife?

These questions may not all seem relevant, but I

assure you that they are realistically based on experience and truly reveal the differences between the town and country minded. Since I came to live in my present home I have been covered with shame by some of my friends who have been fired by my example to leave their street numbers, but have, in a spiritual sense, brought their street with them.

I do not blame them for demanding electric light and a main water supply. There is nothing particularly rustic about a lamp, which is a Victorian method of lighting unknown in country districts until the middle of the last century; and though nothing is more typical of country life than a water shortage there is also nothing more opposed to its main business of farming. What I deplore is their failure to realize that a village is a self-contained and self-sufficing community. The nearest town is for occasions only—a place on the circumference, not the center, of their lives. But invariably they change their orbit and become satellites of the town. There they go shopping, there they refresh themselves with urbanities, with the noises and smell they apparently cannot live without. They even buy their food there. Not long ago I met a woman exhausted after a vain search for bottling plums in the town ten miles away and ignorant of the fact that they heaped the counter of the village shop a few yards from her door. It had not occurred to her that in wartime a country shop was more likely to be supplied with fruit than even the most imposing seaside greengrocer.

A certain bitter piquancy was given to this particular situation by the fortunes of war, which chose the town in question as a favorite target for the tip-and-run raiders. When these raids began I was interested to watch the reactions of various street lovers who up till then had made it a frequent place of pilgrimage. Some of them continued to go as before, apparently finding it superior to the country even if their view of it was almost entirely from an air raid shelter, or—as happened to some—they found themselves thrust by unknown protectors into the coalholes of unknown houses or even more terribly by the butcher into his refrigerator. Others gave up their trips, but wilted and pined in exile; at the first lull they were in the streets again, window-shopping through the foot-square peepholes of the boarded shops.

You say that this is only another example of intolerance over trifles. But I deny that the urbanization of the country is a trifling matter, and I see it acquiring a fresh momentum in the years to come. As the country grows more easily accessible, it is bound to attract many who would otherwise shun it. They will see the chance of enjoying its advantages of peace, beauty and fresh air without having to put up with such disadvantages as retirement and simplicity of life. They will demand and secure amenities, and in the end the countryside, if not disfigured by widespread and inappropriate building, will sink into a sort of *villégiature*, a dormitory for the town, its own indigenous crafts and industries driven into corners where they may survive as "quaint."

This would be an insult as well as a catastrophe. The country is not a place of leisure, for the rest and recreation of the jaded townsman or the evening comfort of the "retired." It is a place of business, of hard work. It is the scene of one of the most vital, most neglected, most maltreated of our national industries. Any great extension of its present occupation by urban fundamentalists would mean the end of farming except as a hobby. Already it is feeling the weight of the invasion, of the loss of good lands, of the starvation of small local markets in favor of large central depots involving endless difficulties in transport and expense. Every farmer suspects that war reliefs in the shape of subsidies and fixed prices are only temporary and are in many cases outweighed by the evils of bureaucracy and ignorant interference from metropolitan high places.

The farming industry's greatest need is a total revision of the nation's outlook toward it. It wants to be put on the same footing as mining or spinning, to have its place in "progressive" political programs instead of being regarded by their protagonists as the symbol of Tory reaction. The cry of "Back to the Land" does not help one whit, as it only looses upon the fields certain of the more romantic and self-deluded town dwellers. The whole things calls for practical legislation. A step in the right direction which could be quickly made would be the forbidding of the diversion of agricultural property to any other purpose whatsoever.

I am well aware that England cannot turn back into the mainly agricultural country that she used to be, that for better, for worse, she is committed to a program of iron and steel and coal, and certainly her present vast population is better broken up and confined in towns than spread over a countryside which it could only submerge in its totality. But to let agriculture sink back into the state it was in before the war would, I am convinced, be a disaster which—apart from any future wars— would in the end affect even the aboriginal city dweller.

There is something in agriculture intrinsic to true civilization, which cannot exist without it, no matter how wide its culture, how deep its plumbing. The day we lose our countryside as a real thing—a working thing, an independent thing, a self-respecting thing—we lose our soul.

9.

I T HAS BEEN SAID OF ST. AUGUSTINE THAT "HIS SERMONS range from the sublimest mysticism to the proper heating of churches." I should be sorry if any thoughts of the great African doctor and of myself should enter the reader's mind at the same time, but perhaps I may use this quotation to sustain my fugue and excuse the fact that in some of my wanderings out of the kitchen I may have wandered too near, for some tastes, to the Church or the House of Commons, neither of which, you may think, is so well heated as the place we have left.

So let us hurry back and end on a comfortable low note, stretching out our hands and our feet to the kitchen fire (ignoring for once the fact that I have only an electric cooker) and listening to the cheerful sound of something bubbling in the pot. That something is the postwar world, considered only as it affects the kitchen. We are giving our minds a rest from Atlantic Charters, the Four Freedoms, the Rights and Wrongs of Small Nations, the Redemption and Re-Selling of Europe, and are merely thinking of the good things we shall make and eat when the good times come back.

One thing that I look forward to with a special glow is the restoration of fish to its old position as a usual, almost conventional article of diet. At present it is more rare than *foie gras* or caviare used to be. For these could always be obtained by anyone who could pay for them, whereas now, for the greater part of the year, even the crown diamonds would not buy a kipper. The epic of the British housewife's adventures in search of fish is one which deserves its place beside other epics of the war, for it is as fine a tale as any of reckless heroism and dogged perseverance. Personally, I do not deserve as high a decoration as some women, for I live at least eight miles from the nearest fish queue. On the other hand, this very remoteness has involved me in troubles unknown to the patient stalactites of the pavement.

Fish, for a country housewife, has been a problem even in peacetime, though when I look back upon those days their difficulties seem no more than the obstacles of a nursery game. Before the war our fish was delivered twice weekly from the seaside town. It came in a special van, with a white-coated fishmonger-driver and lots of ice. The only difficulty it presented was its arrival during my working hours. I used to leave my order beforehand with the cook, instructing her firmly that I should not be interrupted; but no cook of mine seems to have had any just appreciation of the integrity of an author in comparison with the vagaries of a fishmonger. My privacy and diligence were apt to be invaded with sudden cries of—"The fishman hasn't got any sole to-day" or "Would you like kippers for breakfast tomorrow? —he's got some nice ones" or "He's brought some Scotch salmon. Would you rather have that than the turbot?" I protested and appealed but never was I able to secure myself against these interruptions, and bitter was my moaning.

It seems ridiculous now to have made such a fuss, and gladly would I be broken in on every day to save myself the routine by which at last I sometimes (not always by any means) stand possessed of a few fillets of Iceland cod. The first step is to ring up the fishmonger in the seaside town ten miles away, but this is easier said than done. A common reply from the exchange is "junction engaged" and after that there is always "number engaged" to postpone the call to an hour too late for the fish to be put on the ten o'clock bus. This bus is quite the most awkward bus of the day to meet, as it arrives right in the middle of my working hours, always so vulnerable to fish. However, the fishmonger refuses to consider any other, and I must somehow contrive to get into communication with him in the limited time between his opening and the departure of the bus.

If I succeed in doing so, the answer may be a triumphant: "No fish at all this morning," and I must confess to an unworthy feeling of relief when this is so. For there the matter ends. But nearly as often comes the reply—"Only cod fillets" or "Only local plaice." The latter is announced in a tone of apology which is typical of our Sussex methods of self-production. Any North-Countryman or Midlander would answer proudly—"Yes, madam, we've got some beautiful local plaice just come in"—and beautiful it is, fresh and crisp, even after it has gone to and fro all day on the bus, as sometimes happens.

For the process by which it finally arrives in my kitchen has only just begun, and has many points of breakdown. I may decide to lose a part of my working time and meet the bus myself, but more probably I will ask old Fuggle to go, especially if it is a wet day when he will not be more usefully occupied. I tell him to put the fish in the larder and get on with my own work.

At twelve o'clock I go in to cook the fish for lunch. It is not there, and I have to search out old Fuggle, whom I may run to earth at the bottom of the woods or not at all. Anyway, by his statement or by my implication, the fish was not on the bus, so I ring up the fishmonger, who rather angrily states that it was forgotten in the throes of an especially violent queue and that he will put it on the afternoon bus as a great concession.

Meanwhile there is no fish for lunch and I open a tin of Spam—that joke of our lend-lease larder, that butt of B.B.C. comedians, that unfailing laughter raiser of the halls—yet, in my opinion, a grand food, and one I can make utterly delicious with a few cloves and a toffee sauce (equal proportions of margarine and brown sugar). I cannot meet the afternoon bus myself, as I am going out, but Mrs. Boorman will very kindly do this for me. When I come home I read her message on the kitchen slate: "No parcel for you."

The fishmonger is closed now—luckily for him—and there is nothing to do but finish the Spam. The next morning a mysterious and slightly odorous package is on the hall table with the letters. Old Fuggle explains that it was given to him by the postmistress when he went to collect our mail. The bus conductress had brought it in from the last bus the night before. Having denied its existence to Mrs. Boorman, she had discovered the parcel after its second journey from the seaside town, and knowing that old Fuggle collects our letters on his way to work, very resourcefully left it at the postoffice. It is slightly past its prime, but still edible, and we receive it thankfully.

I will not say that all this happens every time I order fish, but some of it nearly always does and the total effect is exhausting. I should fare even worse if it were not for the fact that we are still on an old-fashioned human telephone exchange. The human element takes a sympathetic interest in my struggles and has more than once intervened as the goddess of the machine. After one or two abortive efforts on my part the telephone bell will ring and Mrs. Parker's voice will say—"If you'll hold on I believe I can get your fishmonger for you. I can hear somebody giving an order now and directly she's finished I'll put you on the line." My husband comments truly —"You'd never get an automatic exchange to do *that*."

How shall I feel, I wonder, when all this is over and I can order fish with old-time carelessness and freedom? "A nice Dover sole" . . . or . . . "a pound and a half of Scotch salmon" . . . "a couple of lobsters" . . . or what about "a bit of smoked haddock for breakfast"? . . . all arriving without any superhuman effort on my part in that glistening white van or its postwar successor. I am not expecting any proximate end to my toils in the kitchen, for it is not likely that the millions of empty "situations" throughout the country will be filled by a stampede of maids rushing back to service as fast as they are demobilized. But I look forward to a kitchen less strenuous in its activities, less restricted in raw materials, less makeshift in its equipment, less haunting in its economies.

Even if I could be assured of a good cook the moment life becomes normal—or as near normal as it is ever likely to be—I should still want to have some personal experience of cooking under favorable conditions. I have never yet had a free hand or been able to cook as or what I chose. I have always had to consider scarcities and to be content with substitutes.

I want to make something that is really clever and delicious, not merely a creditable imitation. I am tired of margarine and the "top of the milk." I want to make omelets and cakes with real butter, to put a spoonful of real cream into each egg *en cocotte*. I want to pour a good slosh of maraschino into the fruit salad and to cook strawberries in wine. I am tired of miniature "joints" almost too small to carve and, if one is not to lose all their precious scrap of dripping, involving synthetic gravy. I want to cook a sirloin, with potatoes "under the

·[211]·

roast" from the start instead of being parboiled first in order to be ready at the same time as a pound of animal mystery. I want to make steak and kidney pie of something other than "skirt." I want to make a cake black with fruit and iced with real almond icing instead of a concoction of almond essence and soya flour. I want to make breakfast rolls and waffles dripping with golden syrup. And when I do not feel inclined to cook I want to be able to drive without care for petrol or the police to some well-appointed grillroom and eat a chop or a steak with *pommes allumettes* for half a crown, instead of having to stodge through a typical schoolroom dinner for five shillings and a two shilling cover charge. Or I could enjoy at home that most delicious of all meals—a loaf of crusty homemade bread, real farmhouse butter, and a slice of ham.

10.

So AFTER ALL THIS BOOK ENDS ON A LOW NOTE. I SAID at the beginning that it would be a low book. It might have had as an alternative title *Low Thoughts on Low Living*, and once again I repeat myself to emphasize the conviction that plain living will not, unless sustained by a supernatural impulse, inevitably lead to high thinking. Personally, the fewer good things I have to eat the more I find myself thinking about food, an experience which I believe is shared by arctic explorers, soldiers on the battlefield and in fact by most people who eat only what they can get instead of what they would like.

I would not, however, on any account be without the experiences of the last few years, and I cannot stop writing of them without a grateful salute to the kitchen battlefield for having given me an escape more legitimate than some from that other war which has raged outside its walls at varying degrees of proximity. There have been times when with the German Army barely forty miles away, one could have truthfully said that "you would not know there was a war on." But there have been others when one has realized all the incitement to a good life that lies in the text: "There was silence in heaven for the space of half an hour."

I was not cooking at the time of the 1940 blitz and invasion scare, so I cannot say how firmly my fortress would have held out against the double assault; but it has stood up very well to that later period when the enemy, having thrown everything else at us, finally decided to throw the kitchen stove. For two and a half months objects which I am assured by an engineering friend reflect the greatest credit on the heads of German scientists, if not on their hearts, hurtled noisily over the roof or plunged still more noisily into the surrounding landscape. Occasionally I would withdraw into the air raid shelter, grasping something—say, a piece of raw rabbit—which I should on more deliberate reflection have left behind, and I have even once criminally left the hot plate "on" and the electric kettle blowing its lid off in steam; but in between these lapses my morale has been almost uncannily sustained by such experiments as stewing sausages in beer or making an iced strawberry mousse.

The diversion of the mind into an unfamiliar activity, a secondary yet urgent interest, and the body into a gentle strain, is the best antidote I know to those trials which beset a lonely woman, no longer young, left to deal singlehanded with the marvels of science. One set of marvels as it were cancels out the other, and oh that our scientists would combine to produce only that one set—the marvels which make our homes efficient and comfortable and our labors light, instead of the set which brings them crashing down on our heads. Cannot all the housewives of the world combine to ensure that in future the kitchen stove is used for cooking purposes only?

November, 1943—March, 1945.

Index of Recipes

Set in Linotype Baskerville
Format by A. W. Rushmore
Manufactured by The Haddon Craftsmen
Published by HARPER & BROTHERS
New York and London